ADHD Workbook for Women

Proven Exercises & Strategies to Improve Executive

Functioning, Focus and Motivation. Essential Life Skills

for Women with ADHD

Linda Hill

Table of Contents

Your Included Bonus

Get Your Free 100 ADHD Life Skills Tips with Decluttering Cheat Sheet

We have included a complimentary cheat sheet to go along with this book, which contains a collection of life saving tips from people with ADHD, as well as a home decluttering guide and checklist. This cheat sheet includes tips on:

- Decluttering rooms
- Memory
- Time Blindness
- Distractions

- Sleep
- Relationships
- Work
- School

Get Yours Here: LindaHillBooks.com/adhdtips

Or Scan QR Code:

Introduction

Hello and welcome:

If you are reading this book, you are probably a person with or have a loved one with ADHD. This book is dedicated to all the women who have gone through most of their lives not realizing they have Attention Deficit Hyperactivity Disorder. If you haven't been formally diagnosed yet, but suspect that you have ADHD, you are not alone.

Most women are not diagnosed until their 30s or early 40s (Sreenivas, S. 24 Mar. 2022. "ADHD in Women."). Many theories of why this happens has to do with the social stigma and the role that we must play in the world.

This workbook will break down some of those theories for you, along with exercises that can challenge ADHD symptoms, encourage you to try new things with ADHD, and help you see the power behind your ADHD. It is also a companion piece to the full book Women with ADHD, which came out in July 2022.

If you are a woman with Attention Deficit Hyperactivity Disorder, chances are you weren't diagnosed until you were an adult. If that is the case, you may have difficulty with organization, chores, career, relationships, friendships, and more.

If you are a mom with ADHD, you may feel inadequate, even though you are not. Many women who are mothers report the same thing. Within these pages, you will get to read some of their confessions and see if it sounds like they share the same thoughts as you do.

Society expects a lot out of a woman.

You expect a lot out of yourself.

If you are a wife and mother, you take care of the lives of your family.

If you are single and career-oriented, you work twice as hard as everyone else to show your worth.

If you are somewhere in between, you still provide incredible value to the world, but it is rarely mentioned.

Women do things because they need to be done, not because they are looking for acclaim, props, and credit—although being appreciated is always nice. There may be times when you don't.

Women with ADHD have a greater inclination toward:

- Depression

- Substance Abuse

- Anxiety

- Eating Disorders

- Mood Disorders

- And More

The tendency to backslide into mental issues doesn't mean something is wrong. It means that you are human.

And humanity isn't something women are supposed to have.

While that may sound dramatic, think about how many times you've made excuses for someone else's behavior. Think about how often you've said "I'm sorry" over something small or when you've had a big emotion you're embarrassed about.

Women aren't supposed to cry or be emotional. We aren't supposed to laugh too loud, talk too much, or emote in a way that makes other people uncomfortable. Women are supposed to be quiet—which is where the ADHD diagnosis comes into play and probably why your diagnosis was missed.

ADHD already has a stigma attached to it. Even with all the research, studies, and evidence found within the last twenty years, people still don't know enough about it. What they do know has been based on gender bias.

Even the DSM-IV for the American Psychological Association (APA) has a foundation of ADHD symptoms rooted in male patients. It wasn't until much later, when there was more information on how ADHD affected people, did women and girls start to be considered to have the disorder?

Perhaps you've just recently been diagnosed. How did you feel about the possibility? Did you scoff or question the professional who labeled you? Did you deny that it could even be a possibility? Was ADHD ever on your radar to begin with? Were you shocked that an adult could be diagnosed with the disorder? Did you have a myriad of other reactions that all boil down to the simple idea of disbelief?

Any of those reactions are more common than you realize. And being a woman who is diagnosed with ADHD is becoming a natural occurrence.

The first thing you will have to do, even if you're still in denial about your ADHD, is wash your thoughts of everything you know about it. The current stereotype of adolescent boys climbing over the walls and yelling while they cut their hair off with scissors is just that. It's a stereotype. And while stereotypes are grounded in some myopic truth, most of them are misleading on purpose—so no one looks too closely and finds the chinks in society's armor.

The fact of the matter is that anyone anywhere at any time can be affected by ADHD. This statement also means that anyone, anywhere, anytime, can be diagnosed with ADHD.

Women and girls are the most misdiagnosed people of anyone with ADHD. As it stands, ADHD affects about five percent of adults in the United States (Gatti, 2022). Four out of every ten teachers report having difficulty seeing ADHD in their female students as opposed to their male students (Quinn, 2004).

Undiagnosed or untreated ADHD can cause further complications in a person. Women will be misdiagnosed with mood, personality, or another comorbidity (Kessler, 2004).

A rising number of women from age twenty-four to thirty-six are being diagnosed with ADHD—they are the fastest growing part of the population to get the diagnosis (Kaleidoscope Society, 2022).

So, are you asking yourself, if professionals know this information, why is it still so hard for a woman or girl to get diagnosed with ADHD? The short answer is that ADHD symptoms show themselves differently in women and girls than in boys and men.

The longer answer is that not much research has been studied about gender and ADHD. The diagnosis has been recorded for over 200 years—under different names, of course. Instead of looking at all the symptoms, researchers have focused on the surface-level ones because they are easier to see.

That information doesn't mean that these researchers haven't done a stellar job figuring out a lot about ADHD. It just means that the disorder is so complex that 200 years+ isn't enough to cover all the ways the condition affects people.

Were there gender biases because boys displayed their symptoms in the open and girls and women internalized them? Yes. But now that scientists have discovered the discrepancy, they are working hard to rectify it.

The average woman with ADHD will have symptoms that look like anxiety, depression, and inattention. Women are far better than men at learning how to mask their issues. Women tend to offset traits they believe are inadequate with other tools that lead them to be labeled "perfectionists." This method, while it sounds great, can be maladaptive and unhealthy. If she continues this way, she will not be able to develop healthy coping skills, and her anxiety will skyrocket.

If you're a woman with ADHD, the first thing you'll need to do is to figure out how the symptoms look on you. Acknowledging your issues and owning up to the possible symptoms will only lead you to a place where you feel at peace and set free.

Once you suspect you have ADHD or get diagnosed, you can learn to develop the tools you need to set yourself up for success. Finding a counselor who has experience with ADHD is the best step you can take on the road to helping yourself.

How to Use This Book

This workbook will give you information, data, and exercises to help you hone in on your symptoms and find the right tools and routines. The resources at the back of this workbook will give you other avenues to check out.

The exercises in this book are meant to invoke self-reflection, comfort and ease you into new, healthy habits that will manage your ADHD.

When you read through the book, have a notebook and a pen or pencil to write down thoughts or ideas you may have that help. If you've purchased this book in print, you are free to mark it up, but journaling is still encouraged.

At the end of each section, you will find a space where you can write down your thoughts, introspections, and feelings about the information in the chapter. If you don't know where to begin journaling, you can ask yourself a few questions.

1. What did this chapter tell me?

2. Did I learn anything?

3. Do I like anything more than the other ideas in this chapter?

4. Do I want to incorporate an idea into my routine?

5. How can I integrate an idea/s into my practice?

6. What did I feel when reading through this chapter?

7. How can I organize the thoughts in my mind?

8. How does this chapter relate to my ADHD?

9.   How can I work with my therapist on these exercises?

10.   Do I feel positively or negatively about anything I read?

For question ten, if you find something beneficial or impractical about anything you read, make a note of it. Analyze what about the information that made you feel good, why it made you feel that way, and what you can do about it. If it feels impractical or worthless, you can leave the information in the book and forget about it. However, if the info triggers a distressing reaction, make sure to review it with your therapist.

This workbook is not intended to bring you any tumultuous emotions. Still, anytime you dig into your past and use your feelings while investigating psychological habits, you are bound to have some unpleasantness.

Remember, discomfort and unsavory thoughts mean that you're coming close to unhealthy behavior. These feelings aren't bad, but they are uncomfortable. But if they shift from discomfort to distress, that is a problem you should talk to your therapist about.

The information in this workbook is meant to build a new routine, rewrite the ADHD script, and give you a better outlook on yourself and the world. That doesn't happen without a few bumps and bruises (metaphorical ones), but knowing that you're not alone does make the process much easier.

Pep Talk

You have learned to be resourceful and put others before your progress as a woman. You have adapted to ADHD symptoms and have learned how to mask your issues instead of finding ways to manage them healthily. Yes, you're doing the best you can to survive through the days, but you don't have just to survive. Instead, you can use these exercises and resources to develop helpful, healthy tools that will reroute your ADHD symptoms into a place where you don't feel like you are constantly struggling.

You can release yourself into an easier way of life where you are organized, pay bills on time, and move forward instead of constantly running on a wheel to nowhere.

You are a smart, strong, and intelligent woman.

ADHD does not make you the person you are. It's a neurodivergent development of your brain. It is manageable, and when you learn how to help yourself, you'll see how much more you can help other people, especially those you love.

Although this workbook is a companion piece to the Woman with ADHD book, you'll find exercises that can help you develop new routines, organize your life, and calm the constant chaos inside your chest. You have control over your actions, and by doing the exercises in this book, you're taking control back (or maybe for the first time) and getting the life you want and deserve to live.

However, working through ADHD is not going to be easy. Think about how long you've had the habits ingrained inside of you. It will take time to erase them. Don't worry if you struggle at first. Although it doesn't feel good, the struggle signifies movement and change. Don't worry if things feel uncomfortable—they will. But discomfort isn't a bad thing. It means you're doing things differently than you have in the first place.

You will have days when anxiety and negative self-talk. You will have days where everything falls into place, and you will have more days in between. Even when it seems as though everything is going wrong, tell yourself you're doing it right—because you are doing something to help yourself.

That's all you need.

This book will help you create a solid connection with your ADHD. It will guide you away from bad habits and encourage the acceptance of your entire self.

By looking at the ADHD community of women, you'll find that you're not alone. And if you aren't sure where to start, know I'm right here with you.

We're going to get through this together.

CHAPTER ONE

What is ADHD?

Introduction

Reading this book, you probably already know what ADHD is. However, a brief overview of ADHD can be helpful to refresh your memory and provide a reference if needed.

This chapter will review ADHD and give you some exercises to help you determine what your symptoms are and what type of ADHD you may have. These exercises are in no way a formal diagnosis but a guide to help you find the best treatment plans and solutions to fit your lifestyle.

Throughout this book, you will be reminded that finding professional help from a therapist or psychiatrist who has experience with ADHD is going to be a tremendous asset to you and your plight.

What is ADHD?

ADHD is a neurodevelopmental difference in the way your brain works. People without ADHD, mood disorders, or chemical imbalances have neurotypical brains. Those with ADHD are considered to have neurodivergent brains. When your brain has ADHD, it has not only developed different, but the network of neurons, synapses, and chemicals does not work in the way that a neurotypical brain does—this creates a problem because even though your brain is neurodivergent, any human brain needs certain things to work in a streamlined way.

Instead, your brain is starved of chemicals and hormones like dopamine, the synapse misfires, and the network doesn't run smoothly.

This development creates a lot of issues for those with ADHD, especially if they don't know what is going on.

There are three types of ADHD:

- **Inattentive**—when you have inattentive ADHD, you will have trouble finishing, paying attention to, and organizing tasks. You can have problems following conversations or listening to instructions. You probably find that you're easily distracted and even forget about daily routines. This type of ADHD is one of the most common for women, and the quiet nature of the disorder is one of the main reasons girls are not diagnosed in school.

- **Hyperactive/Impulsive**—although it may sound surprising, this type of ADHD is the least common. It is more well-known because the symptoms are louder, larger, and more impulsive. If you have this type of ADHD, you will have trouble sitting still or talking for a long time. You may often react impulsively and feel restless at the same time. You may have loved jumping, climbing, screaming, and running around. Impulsiveness will have you interrupt conversations, grab things, and speak over others. You are probably more prone to accidents and injuries than the average person (Centers for Disease Control and Prevention, 26 Jan. 2021. "What Is ADHD?").

- **Combination**—unsurprisingly, you may realize that the combination type of ADHD is the most common. You could have several symptoms from each category, which makes ADHD unique for each person. (Centers for Disease Control and Prevention, 26 Jan. 2021. "What Is ADHD?").

Exercise One—What Are My Symptoms?

Check off the symptoms that seem to fit your personality and traits. Review the symptoms below to see what type of ADHD matches most with your answers.

- Have problems following through on duties for your job?

- Talk too much.

- Have been accused of not listening during conversations.

- Interrupts other conversations, games, activities, etc., without being asked to join. Alternatively, you may take over an activity completely to avoid having to give instructions or explain yourself.

- Have issues organizing your day—cannot manage time well. You often miss deadlines or have been told your work is disorganized or messy.

- Need to be "on the go" constantly.

- Have an inability to stay seated at work.

- Are unable to do quiet activities.

- Have issues with focus, such as staying on task or finishing activities, especially during conversations, reading, and lectures.

- Dislike or avoid projects that may require continued mental effort, like completing forms and preparing reports.

- Often lose important items that you need daily. Items like cellphones, glasses, keys, wallets, etc.

- You forget daily tasks like chores, errands, keeping appointments, paying bills, and returning phone calls.

- Have issues sitting still. Often jiggles feet or hands, shifts in your seat, or fidgets.

- You become distracted easily.

- Can't pay attention to details and make careless mistakes at your job.

- You cannot seem to wait for someone to finish asking a question before you complete their sentences or answer. You cannot wait to speak.

(Davis, Sarah, and Linda Hill. 2022. Women with ADHD: The Complete Guide to Stay Organized, Overcome Distractions, and Improve Relationships. Manage Your Emotions, Finances, and Succeed in Life.)

Symptoms

Inattentiveness

- You can't pay attention to details and make careless mistakes at your job.

- Have issues with focus, such as staying on task or finishing activities, especially during conversations, reading, and lectures.

- Have problems following through on duties for your job.

- Have been accused of not listening during conversations.

- Have issues organizing your day—cannot manage time well. You often miss deadlines or have been told your work is disorganized or messy (Psychiatry.org. Accessed Aug. 13, 2022. "What is ADHD?").

- Dislike or avoid projects that may require continued mental effort, like completing forms and preparing reports.

- Often lose important items that you need daily. Items like cellphones, glasses, keys, wallets, etc.

- You become distracted easily.

- You forget daily tasks like chores, errands, keeping appointments, paying bills, and returning phone calls (CDC. Jan. 26, 2021) (Davis, S. 2022).

Hyperactivity or Impulsiveness

- Have issues sitting still. Often jiggles feet or hands, shifts in your seat, or fidgets.

- Have an inability to stay seated at work.

- Need to be "on the go" constantly.

- Talk too much.

- Are unable to do quiet activities.

- You cannot seem to wait for someone to finish asking a question before you complete their sentences or answer. You cannot wait to speak.

- Interrupts other conversations, games, activities, etc., without being asked to join. Alternatively, you may take over the activity completely to avoid having to give instructions or explain yourself (Psychiatry.org. Accessed Aug. 13, 2022.),(CDC. Jan. 26, 2021), (Davis, S. 2022).

When you tally your score, check to see if you have five or more answers. If you do, compare your marks with Inattentive or Hyperactive/Impulsive symptoms. Your responses will give you a better idea of your ADHD type and how to begin to build your treatment plan. When you take your answers to your medical professional, you'll be able to tackle your symptoms one by one.

If you find that you have several from each section—inattentive and hyperactive—you will probably be diagnosed with Combination ADHD and can develop a treatment plan from several angles.

If you have not been formally tested, doing so is a good idea. You'll need to find a therapist or medical professional to perform the test. ADHD is not discovered through blood work. Instead, you'll take a series of paper tests, hearing and vision screenings, and interviews that will take a few days to complete.

Once you are formally diagnosed (or just suspect you have ADHD), you can begin to look at treatments (Davis, S. 2022).

Treatments

Once you realize that you have ADHD, a golden door of opportunities does open up for you. Again, that may sound a little melodramatic, but putting a label on your struggles gives you a map of how to help yourself. When that happens, a weight can be lifted off of your shoulders.

After you've figured out what kind of ADHD type you have, inattentive, hyperactive-impulsive, or combination, you can begin to focus on a plan that will spotlight the most beneficial way to live your best life. You can literally find out how your brain works. It's a pretty cool process.

One caveat, although it happens more often in children transitioning into adulthood, is that sometimes symptoms morph into others. If you start with hyperactivity and find good ways to maneuver your brain in the right way, your brain may overcorrect and shift you into an inattentive form of ADHD. That doesn't mean you can work with those symptoms, but it is something to keep in the back of your mind. This is a possibility (Psychiatry Org, Aug 2022).

This information is not meant to discourage you. Instead, think of it as a post-it note reminding you that while ADHD is manageable and you can retrain your brain to create better habits and function properly, it may never go away completely. The human brain can be pretty persnickety in that way, but if you notice some oddities in your behavior once you've tackled one set of symptoms, you may need to go in and create a few modifications to combat the next type.

Treatment plans usually do include a combination of behavioral therapy and medication. However, your specific plan will depend on what your lifestyle requires, what your symptoms are, and where your comfort level lies.

No matter what plan you and the medical professional come up with, it is your plan. You have to be comfortable with it—this statement is different than getting comfortable being uncomfortable. This statement has more to do with your gut. If you don't feel that an aspect of your plan doesn't fit into your beliefs, methods, lifestyle, etc., you need to express it to your therapist.

However, if you believe that you are simply afraid of trying something new, you should also be aware of that. To find out if you are worried or if it is an attack on your core values, you should ask yourself a few questions.

Exercise Two—Developing a Treatment Plan I'm Comfortable With

Think about what your responses would be to the ten questions below. Write out or journal your answers to give you a better idea of what you're comfortable with and what is an absolute non-starter. There is space below to write your answers, or you can do it in a separate notebook.

1.   What am I avoiding?

2.   Am I just afraid of this new process?

3.   Do I think my therapist would steer me in the wrong direction?

4.   Do I trust my therapist?

5.   Do I trust myself?

6.   How can this method help me?

7.   How can this method hurt me?

8.   Am I just not ready to try the process?

9.   Do I not want to try something new because it is unfamiliar to me?

10.   Will I be hurting myself (metaphorically) if I don't try it?

So, how do you know if you have a good treatment plan?

A plan that will be beneficial for your ADHD will have you and your therapist monitoring your actions, thoughts, and behaviors closely. You'll have follow-up sessions to discuss what is working and what routines need to be changed. While a therapist is not necessary, finding someone that works with you is an incredibly healthy and helpful resource.

One of the goals of this workbook is to help you manage your systems. However, by going through the book and talking to a therapist, spiritual leader, or another medical professional, you're giving yourself an extra boost of assistance.

The main thing to remember when building your treatment plan is that you're doing this for a better life.

Before developing a treatment plan, you'll have to understand your goals for the program. The next exercise will help you do this.

What are Treatment Goals?

Think about this question. You can develop your treatment goals in several ways. However, because you have ADHD, make sure you use SMART goals. The SMART goal method includes: Specific, Measurable, Attainable, Relevant, and Timely goals (Stewart, Sept. 2021; Main, 2021).

With ADHD, it's good to have a BIG goal in your mind—where you see yourself in three, five, and ten years. But it's equally important, if not more so, to have goals you can break into chunks to complete and accomplish things.

When you incorporate SMART goals into your practice, you're giving yourself smaller goals on your way to working toward bigger goals, and then you can focus on the even larger-scaled goals. You can think of it like stairs, a pyramid, or something else more fun for you. But each time you knock on one of your smaller goals, you've walked up another step.

For your SMART goals, you're going to want to write them down. Most ADHD types do better when they have a visual aid—hence why it is important to have a notebook along with this book. You can use it as a constant reference.

Think about your goals. What is the result you're looking for when managing your ADHD?

An example can be: *I want to have a routine where I wake up every morning, work out, go to my job, come home, clean for twenty minutes, walk the dog, make dinner, and then spend three hours with my family.*

Now, that example is very specific and doesn't have to be that detailed. But it can be. If you don't know what you want your end goal with the ADHD treatment plan to be, that is okay too. You can take it one day at a time.

The sky is limitless to what works best for you.

If you would prefer to know your goal but don't know how to get there—close your eyes and envision who you are and what you are doing in three months, then six, then one year. What does each one of those images look like?

Write it down.

When you have those visions written down, ask yourself where they will lead. Are you looking to become a novelist? Do you want to learn to play the cello? Do you want to run a marathon? Be the president of the PTA?

Once you have a few goals written down, incorporate the SMART method for each one. This method is to help you find short-term success toward your long–term goals.

Exercise Three—What are My Treatment Goals?

Goal: Write down your long-term plan below.

_____

_____

_____

Goals: Break your long-term goal into five short-term goals. Use the SMART Method.

Short-Term Goal

_____

_____

_____

Instructions: Fill out your particular actions below to meet the short-term goal.

Specific—

A specific goal lets you narrow down the idea into one action. You can start with an action word to use in your sentences.

Example: Plan, organize, implement, develop, transform, meditate, run, ride, clean, etc.

Think about these things before or as you are writing:

1. What is your mission?

2. What are the specific terms of the goal? (Steer clear of describing how you will accomplish your goal).

3. Answer Who, What, Where, When, and Why (Stewart, Becca. 23 Sept. 2021).

_____

_____

_____

_____

_____

_____

Measurable—

With your specific goal in mind, explain how you will determine that your particular purpose is complete. What benchmarks do you reach to feel that you've accomplished your plan? Don't be general. Make sure to use as much detail as you can muster up.

This goal should be attainable, realistic, and quantitative.

_____

_____

_____

_____

_____

_____

Achievable—

Is your goal realistic? Given your skills, capabilities, level of control, etc., can you reach this goal?

If you find that your goal is to be a pop star, that's a great goal—but it is not a short-term achievable goal until you've already had agents lining up to get your signature on a billion-dollar contract. Instead, you could start by setting your goal toward doing the best you can in public. Alternatively, get three singing gigs for three weekends in a row.

To find out if your goal is achievable, ask yourself the following questions:

1. How heavily does the success of this goal rely on others? Do you only rely on yourself?

2. Do you have time to reach this goal? If not, are you willing to make time?

3. Is the goal possible within the scheduled deadline?

4. Are the parameters too tight or too loose?

5. Will you need help reaching your goal? Who will be the person or people to help you?

6. If you can complete your plan alone, how will you do it?

_____

_____

_____

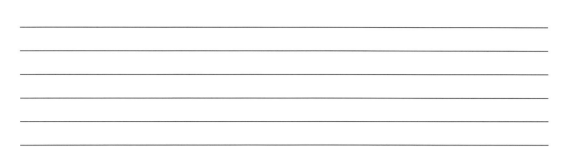

There is no need to spread yourself too thin in any manner. When people try to accomplish goals, they fail because they have strained themselves physically, mentally, emotionally, and financially.

If you burn out before you reach your goal, you might have a harder time reaching it. Or, the worst-case scenario is that you will give it up. Don't give up if you feel like your dreams are too big or may stretch your abilities right now. Instead, revisit the Specific goal and rewrite it. You can develop something that won't break your bank, spirit, or body (Stewart, Becca. 23 Sept. 2021).

Relevant—

Is your specific goal relevant to your long-term goal?

If you want to be a pop star and your goal right now is to get a car, think about how those two goals connect. Do you want to get a car so you have freedom and independence to go on tour in different cities, or is your goal less connected? It may sound a little weird, but these things matter when planning your short-term goals, especially when you have ADHD (Stewart, Becca. 23 Sept. 2021).

To find out if your goal is relevant to your long-term one, answer the questions below:

1. Does your plan make sense based on what you're already doing?

2. Can you make these changes right now?

3. Does your strategy match the larger purpose of your long-term goals?

4. Does your plan align with your professional and personal values?

If you've answered 'no' to these questions, you should rework your specific goals a little more.

_____

_____

_____

_____

_____

_____

_____

_____

Timely—

Have you given yourself a deadline? If not, make sure to add that to the goal. While you can complete the plan quicker than the scheduled time you set out for yourself, make sure it is a realistic timeframe. Don't put it so close that you cannot achieve it, but don't put it so far away that you don't feel like you need to rush on it.

Usually, a goal of three weeks is an admirable timeline. If you don't think that you can achieve your goal at this time or cannot move things around in your schedule for it—you'll have to look at the plan you set out for yourself and probably rework it a little.

The point of the SMART method is to help you learn how to achieve small-term goals in a realistic amount of time. If you can fit your goal into a timeframe or cannot maneuver it around your schedule, your goal may be too big to be specific.

Write down your deadline. Also, add why it is a realistic timeframe so you understand if it is enough, too much, or just the right amount of time for you (Stewart, Becca. 23 Sept. 2021).

_____

_____

_____

_____

_____

_____

Exercise Four—Acting on My Treatment Goals

Remember that this section concerns your behavioral and medical treatment plans and goals. When you act on those goals, you will need some tools to help keep you motivated. This next exercise will give tips to help you follow through with your goals and help you hold yourself accountable when you do not.

● **Write down your goals**. An article in Psychology Today discussed how writing your goals down can achieve thirty-three percent higher culpability. In the article, Marilyn Price-Mitchell also discovered:

"Research has uncovered many key aspects of goal-setting theory and its link to success (Kleingeld et al., 2011). Setting goals is linked with self-confidence, motivation, and autonomy (Locke & Lathan, 2006)."

When you write down your goals, keep them in a familiar area so you can look at them often and be reminded of them. If you have any ADHD, this tip is a helpful one to keep the goals at the forefront of your mind.

● **Share your ideas and goals with your family or friends**. Many people are a little gun-shy about this particular tip. Sharing your thoughts with others can leave you feeling open to vulnerability. However, when you share parts of yourself with the people who love and care about you, they should support it. They may even help you figure out how to do things better.

● **Visualize your results**. Professionals, especially athletes and performers, use visualization to walk through the motions of them doing their job flawlessly. Through this vision, they will also reach their ideal outcome (basketball players want to get the ball in the net, singers want to put on a dynamite show). A vision board is a great way to make your goals real.

If you are not ready to create a vision board (more on this later), you can close your eyes and see yourself completing your desired result.

● **Revisit your goals—a lot**. Make sure to check in with your goals frequently. Once you do this, you can track your progress and see where there may need to be some changes. As you grow and develop your treatment plan, what was important to you may no longer grow to be. However, that does not mean you stop wanting things, and it does not mean that you should stop making goals. Change things as needed, and you will find that your goals are still achievable.

Examples of Treatment Goals

If you are still having trouble coming up with goals for your treatment, read the list below to see if there is something familiar you can take and use until you get into the habit of forming goals. Below is a list of example goals, andspace to do some writing, or make sure to use your notebook to brainstorm your thoughts after you read the sample goals (Stewart, Becca. 23 Sept. 2021).

- Learn to be less distracted by voices and music when I am in public.

- Learn how to accept myself.

- Learn how to discuss my ADHD struggles confidently.

- Create an exercise regime.

- Find out more about ADHD

- Find out more about my hormones

- How do I motivate my mind when I am distracted?

- Discover more about Executive Function and how I can improve it.

- Learn about Object Permanence and how it applies to ADHD.

- How can I organize my home to fit with my ADHD?

- Schedule work and processing time.

- Enlist people who love and care about me to help.

- Learn more about ADHD and social habits.

- Learn more about ADHD and my sex life.

- Find out how to be more compassionate with my children.

- Discover how to use mindfulness in my ADHD routines.

Healthy Living

One of the best ways to begin your ADHD treatment plan is to get into a healthy mindset. Think about how you treat your body. What kinds of food do you eat? Do you exercise? How do you sleep? What activities do you enjoy doing? Regardless of your neurological makeup, when you treat your body healthily and respectfully, it works better. Clean food and five hours a week of activity will help release beneficial chemicals into your brain to help it work with less stuttering. While we will discuss healthier living in a later chapter, below are some quick tips to get you started.

- **Discover a healthier way to eat**: look at your eating habits—are they good, moderate, bad, or unhealthy? The only person you have to be honest with yourself about this is you. You know if there are times when you binge eat a package of Oreos or if you mostly eat clean foods and whole grains. You know. Nevertheless, when you eat bad stuff, even if it tastes incredible, that moment of blissful eating only lasts a short while.

Processed foods, white bread, and refined sugars affect your body differently. If you do not think so, make sure you start to keep a food diary of how you feel after you eat healthily versus how you feel if you eat garbage food.

You will not be able to switch all your bad habits at once. And no one is asking you to; however, if you take small steps toward eating healthy—such as finding one healthy food that you enjoy eating or finding recipes that might be good—then you are making progress. You are not doing this to lose weight; you are doing it to help your body work better.

- **Make time for three to five hours of weekly exercise or physical activity.** Find activities you like and want to do. Once you get into a good workout, change your routine so you do not get bored.

One hour a day is a fantastic way to burn up some excess ADHD energy and keep you going in the long run.

As you work out, you will feel better because endorphins and cortisol are released more frequently into your system. These are great chemicals that help your body work at its highest capacity. The more you engage in physical fitness, the better tuned in you are going to be. The more tuned in you get with it, the more you will be able to manage your ADHD.

- **Find out about sleeping better.** Different age groups need different amounts of sleep—however, studies have found that sleep gives your body and mind the time it needs to rest. It also cleanses your body of toxins your brain picks up throughout the day, and several areas of your brain will change their activity level between sleeping and waking.

In these times, your molecular mechanisms will clear away a lot of gathered dirt and debris that will slow your brain down and will replenish your brain with cleaner, newer chemicals like melatonin, GABA, adenosine, and more (Healthy Sleep. Harvard Med. Accessed 14, Aug. 2022. "Why Do We Sleep, Anyway?"), (National Institute of Neurological Disorders and Stroke. Accessed 14 Aug. 2022. "Brain Basics: Understanding Sleep), (Davis, S. 2022.)

- **Watch your screen time.** Careers that work with computers may make using this tip a little more tricky than it can seem at first glance. We are all told to keep our screen time low, but it is hard to do with e-books, phones, tablets, and laptops.

If you find it difficult to start with this tip, just stay away from a screen for one hour before you go to bed to see how your sleep works.

To keep yourself from checking your phone, put it away at night before lying down. You can do this by putting it on a charging station that is not in your bedroom or farther away from your bed.

If that does not work, try to take short breaks each hour to give your brain, eyes, and body a rest from screens.

Conclusion

Attention Deficit Hyperactivity Disorder has some unique traits and hurdles to jump over, but with practice, determination, and kindness for yourself, you'll be able to get through anything.

CHAPTER TWO

Women & ADHD

Introduction

In the companion book Women with ADHD (Davis and Hill, 2022), there is a discussion about how to accept your diagnosis. Whether at first, you may think that the doctor is wrong or that a veil to a deeper part of yourself has been lifted, your process will begin with acceptance.

First, you'll have to do a few things:

- **Accept**—Your brain chemistry doesn't mean there is anything wrong, broken, or bad with how your brain works.

- **Accept**—ADHD does not define you. ADHD is part of your identity, but it is not the only thing.

- **Accept**—Even without ADHD, life will continue to have its ups and downs. Now, with practice, routine, and solutions, you may be able to manage those rollercoaster moments a little bit more.

- **Accept**—you will still get stressed. ADHD will still get in the way, but how you talk about it can help you flip your feelings around.

Exercise Five: Learning About Your Acceptance and Denial

This exercise will flex your ability to reframe the dialogue you have with yourself. Inner dialogue can be incredibly invasive and can lead you down a rabbit hole of dissatisfaction and untruths about yourself.

What would you say if you took a step away from the negative self-talk in your head and instead talked to and about yourself as you would if you were speaking to a friend? How would you give this advice?

If you call yourself dumb, stupid, or an idiot—or allude to it from an action you make. For example, if you made a simple mistake by misplacing your keys and muttering, "I'm such an idiot," to yourself. Would you tell your friend they are an idiot if they lost their keys, or would you tell them that it happens to everyone?

Instructions:

1. Write down actions that have occurred.

2. Include what you THINK about yourself when it happens.

3. Be as brutal as your mind is.

Don't do this to be mean to yourself, but to see how wonky your brain works. When you visualize the words you say to yourself, you will see how unforgiving you are about ADHD.

Underneath the unforgiving statement, write a different phrase about the same experience, only this time, pretend you are speaking to a friend. Do you see how you talk to yourself differently than speak to others? Once you know the difference, it will be time to give a more positive, forgiving, and reframed statement to yourself about your ADHD and actions that may relate to your diagnosis.

1. What Happened?

_____

_____

_____

_____

What did your inner dialogue say?

_____

_____

_____

_____

What would you say to a friend?

_____

_____

_____

_____

2. **What Happened?**

_____

_____

_____

_____

What did your inner dialogue say?

_____

_____

_____

_____

What would you say to a friend?

_____

_____

_____

_____

3. What Happened?

_____

_____

_____

_____

What did your inner dialogue say?

_____

_____

_____

_____

What would you say to a friend?

_____

_____

_____

_____

4. What Happened?

_____

_____

_____

What did your inner dialogue say?

_____

_____

_____

_____

What would you say to a friend?

_____

_____

_____

_____

5. What Happened?

_____

_____

_____

_____

What did your inner dialogue say?

_____

_____

_____

_____

What would you say to a friend?

_____

_____

_____

_____

Once you get into good practice with reframing, you'll find it easier to forgive yourself for little mistakes, and your negative self-dialogue will shift into a more positive light.

Nikki Kinzer, a certified ADHD coach and podcast host from the organization _Take Control of ADHD_, says:

"Before you can fully accept your ADHD, it's important to understand your ADHD. Many clients are surprised when I tell them it's not them; it's ADHD. It's very difficult to separate what's ADHD and what's not. The more you learn about it, the better (Kinzer, 2022)."

The key takeaways Kinzer encourages are:

- You are not broken.

- You do not need to be fixed.

- It's a process to shed the shame and stigma around ADHD; there are a lot of misconceptions of what it is and isn't, but think about how it would feel to accept yourself regardless of how the ADHD shows up (Kinzer, 2022).

Why Didn't Anyone Know?

You may ask yourself, why didn't anyone know or suspect your ADHD before you became diagnosed?

There are a few reasons:

- First, ADHD tests have synonymously been male-forward. Only over the past twenty years have girls been included in trials, research, and studies. DSM-V still only has symptoms that relate to male test subjects instead of using the more inclusive signs found in all genders (Sarkis, 2011).

- Next, women and girls can be misdiagnosed. Because ADHD presents itself differently in females than in males, ADHD can be diagnosed as anything from depression to bipolar (ADDitude Editors and Littman, 2022; Low and Lakhan, 2022).

- Researchers at the National Libraries of Medicine (NIH) conducted a study on "Females with ADHD." They developed a theory called "the female protective effect," This theory surmises that women (and girls) have a higher threshold of external stimuli for their ADHD to come out (Young et al., 2020; Taylor et al., 2016; Davis et al., 2022).

Sarah Ludwig Rausch, a journalist, ADHD advocate, and woman with ADHD, shares her experience before and after her diagnosis in her article, "So That's Why I Found My Phone in the Fridge Again (2022)!"

Rauch dictates her discovery not because she had problems in her life but because she noticed that a reader of her work listed the symptoms that led the reader to get tested for ADHD. When Rauch read about the reader's symptoms, she stated, "It was like I was reading about my own life (Rausch)." Her article details a list of things that seem like innocent mistakes, but when stacked up daily, they can lead to stress, frustration, and poor life management.

"Late for everything? Check.

Always losing your phone/keys/other important items? Check.

Difficulty focusing? Constantly putting off work that takes a lot of concentration? Completely disorganized despite your best efforts?

Check, check, and check (Rausch)."

Many women with ADHD feel that something is missing; if they could just figure out what it is, everything else would fall into place. While getting your ADHD diagnosis can be the missing key, rewriting the ADHD script will be a little harder than sliding a key into a lock and turning. Instead, you will have to unwind each part of your ADHD and start at the beginning. Discover what the triggers are and where your barriers lie. To do that, you will become more self-reflective and learn to get comfortable with some uncomfortable situations.

Breaking the Barriers of ADHD

The previous statement about getting comfortable with uncomfortable situations does not mean that you (or we) will be putting yourself in harm's way. It means that you will have some discomfort through self-reflection and redirecting habits because the new practices are something you have not done before.

Think about a friend (or yourself) who has "tried" something for a few days or even weeks, but they eventually give it up because "it did not work for them" or "they did not like it." Unfortunately, there is a high possibility that they just were not comfortable with the process. The other option is that they really didn't like the experience, which is a fine line you will also have to figure out. It's important to listen to your instincts, but pushing against barriers you've built up for yourself to protect your mind and emotions from ADHD symptoms is equally important.

For example, you do not like watching sports. You especially don't like watching them on television. If you are at a stadium, you would much rather be walking around looking at things than sitting there watching people perform feats of strength against each other while a mascot tries to get me to pander to them along with the rest of the crowd. No amount of rewriting your ADHD brain will make you like sports—this type of entertainment just isn't for you.

If you have moments where your emotions spike because they get triggered by losing keys and being late to take my son to baseball practice, where you wind up snapping at him because you hate sports, that is something you can rewrite. First, it is not your son's fault that you do not like sports, lost your keys, or are overwhelmed by having to take him to practice when nothing is going right. Honestly? It is not your fault, either.

Your ADHD symptoms have been how you have functioned for most of your life, if not your whole life. It can't be unwritten with the click of your fingers.

Think about the several things that can be rewritten in the latter example of getting overwhelmed. Before you think that there is no way to do it, remember that there is always a way to build healthier habits for a more organized lifestyle.

The first step that you will have to take is to discover how your ADHD symptoms affect your daily life. Then you will have to come up with a plan so you can begin to rework, rewrite, and reflect on how you look at ADHD, daily tasks, bigger projects, and more.

Exercise Six: What Everyday Stressors Are ADHD Symptoms

List your daily actions below. Anything you question about yourself, like "Why cannot I {insert chosen responsibility, example, issue, etc.}?" or "Why don't I {insert chosen responsibility, example, issue, etc.}?"

Chances are, if you try your damndest to get something situated but still cannot manage to do so, it is probably part of your ADHD. See examples below for a better idea of tackling this exercise. The purpose of getting your symptoms down and out is to realize and recognize how your brain sometimes works against you, despite how often and hard you try. When you recognize your symptoms are separate from your person, it is much easier to view things with kindness and come up with the best plan of action to shift gears.

Examples:

- I always forget where I put my keys—even if I try to put them in a designated area.

- I set my alarm so I could show up to work on time, but I still managed to be twenty minutes late.

- Even with a list for the grocery store, I find so many interesting items. I always go way over my budget.

Your Turn:

- _____

- _____

- _____

- _____

- _____

- _____

- _____

- _____

- _____

- _____

- _____

- _____

- _____

- _____

- _____

- _____

- _____

- _____

Once you complete this exercise, sit down and reflect on what your ADHD symptoms are. If you see a pattern or habit, you can start to build a plan that will help you correct or redirect the issue.

Exercise Six: Mindfulness Breathing

Mindfulness breathing can help you with many things, especially stress, anxiety, and big emotions caused by traumatizing moments. This type of thinking, breathing, and other exercises will be discussed throughout the workbook. Mindfulness breathing can also help you start to recognize where, when, and why your ADHD symptoms appear.

Mindful breathing is a practice you can do anytime, anywhere. When you use this breathing regularly, your stress levels lower, your thoughts will be clearer, and you will have an overall sense of calmness (Celestine, 2022).

Mindful breathing will give you a gentle focus on your breath. Pay attention to the air coming in and out of your nose and mouth. Do not try to change your breathing. You have no expectations about how to do it. Instead, you are simply aware of your breath from moment to moment.

Even if you do not realize it, when you breathe with mindful intentions, you are in a state of meditation. Other meditative practices involve concentration at the present moment. This consideration will include what you are thinking, feeling, and sensing right as you breathe in and out.

You will not judge thoughts, feelings, senses, or actions in this practice. You will just be.

Deep breathing exercises link the benefits of deep breathing to mindfulness to help you cope better with stressful or triggering times.

Instructions: Practice this exercise when you wake up, before you go to bed, or whenever you begin to feel anxious, stressed, or targeted for rejection. To apply mindful breathing to your routine, do the following:

1. From your seated or standing position, inhale on the count of four.

2. Hold your breath for the count of three.

3. Exhale on the count of four.

4. Repeat five to ten times.

If you prefer a different position or perspective, try the exercise below in the morning after you wake up or just before you go to bed.

- Stand up straight, then bend at the waist.

- Dangle your arms close to the floor.

- Inhale slowly for a count of three.

- Return to a standing position by rolling up slowly. Lift your head last.

- Hold your breath for a count of four.

- Exhale your breath for a count of five.

- As you exhale, slowly bend over again with your hands above your head and dangling at the side of your arms.

- Repeat for three cycles.

- Reflect on how you feel afterward—pay attention to your mind, body, and emotions (Celestine, 2022).

By working on mindfulness breathing in these moments, you are teaching your brain to behave differently.

This workbook will touch on mindfulness exercises more in later chapters. However, if you are interested in looking up other types of mindfulness, read the list below. The practices below can be structured or unstructured:

- Pay attention.

- Accept yourself.

- Live in the moment.

- Bring your focus to your breathing.

- Sitting meditation.

- Meditative walking.

- Body scan meditation (Mayo Clinic Staff, 2020).

When you are asked to **pay attention**, it may seem like a simple request. However, this practice takes focus. It also requires you to slow down your brain, body, and emotions to meet the moment. Paying attention will have you participate right where you are at. You will engage all senses—sight, smell, sound, taste, and touch—as they happen. This exercise will not have you experiencing something on a grand scale. For example, if you are watching a baseball game, instead of watching the entire game, take time to notice what the pitcher is doing, what actions the second-base player is doing, how the grass looks on the field, and what the stadium around you sounds like, etc. (Mayo Clinic Staff, 2020).

While a baseball game may be a grand example, the point of the exercise will be to remove yourself from the event and observe the action. Your goal would be to focus on one thing at a time and give yourself that one thing full attention.

This type of mindfulness will help you retrain your brain into a different way of focusing.

Accepting yourself can be a difficult task to master, and even if you have finally accepted yourself for who you are, you will find that there will be days when you still aren't as kind as you could be.

However, each time you recognize that you are engaging in negative self-talk or self-deprecation, ask yourself, "Would I say this to anyone else?" And instead, think of how you would talk to your friend if they went through or experienced the same thing— don't think about what you should have said or could have done. Accept that the moment happened as it did, and the only thing you can do about it is to learn from it. Before learning from it, you must be nice to yourself, talk to yourself as if you are your best friend, and remind her that it is okay to make mistakes. For example, if you went to a baseball game because you thought it would be fun, then realized that you hate baseball, what would you say to yourself?

To **live in the moment** is similar to paying attention. However, with this mindfulness practice, you will find enjoyment in the moment you are paying attention to (Mayo Clinic Staff, 2020). If, for example, you're back at that baseball game and the sun is warm and shining on you, soak in the warmth. Instead, savor the snack in a way you have not before if you are eating a box of popcorn.

Exercise Seven: Examples of Living in the Moment (LITM)

Instructions: Think about ten things that you really enjoy. Write down why you enjoy them and how they make you feel. Then, when you get a chance, do one of those things. Make sure to pay attention to what is going on and live in the moment—you can even come back to the book and write down how your experience changed.

Example Moment: I really like to read books.

Explanation LITM: When I read, I am at my own time and pace. I connect to myself in a way I do not normally. I love the feeling of turning pages like I am accomplishing something. If I am lying in bed, the blankets are cozy, and the pillow cushions my head. I remind myself to inhale and exhale during quiet moments of the story and realize I am holding my breath during a tenser moment.

1.   Moment One:

_____

_____

Explanation LITM:

_____

_____

2.   Moment One:

_____

_____

Explanation LITM:

_____

_____

3.   Moment One:

_____

_____

Explanation LITM:

_____

_____

4.   Moment One:

_____

_____

Explanation LITM:

_____

_____

5.   Moment One:

_____

_____

Explanation LITM:

_____

_____

6.   Moment One:

_____

_____

Explanation LITM:

_____

_____

_____

7.   Moment One:

_____

_____

Explanation LITM:

_____

_____

8.   Moment One:

_____

_____

Explanation LITM:

_____

_____

9.   Moment One:

_____

_____

Explanation LITM:

_____

_____

10.   Moment One:

_____

_____

_____

Explanation LITM:

_____

_____

After you get into a good habit of living in the moment, you can make it a planned experience or discover that it begins to happen spontaneously. Make sure to remind yourself to do it every once in a while. It is a great way just to reset yourself when you need to.

If you are looking to delve into deeper meditation types that are still easy to do, even while you are working, try some of the below meditative mindfulness exercises to see if you would like to look into them even further.

Sitting meditation will have you sit in a chair. While you should have quiet time, you can be at work and take a five-minute break to engage in your meditative state. Sit with your back straight, feet flat on the ground, and hands in your lap. The most important part of this position is to make sure you are comfortable. You will not want to move. Instead, you will focus on breathing. You will move your breath in and out of your body. When your thoughts or physical feelings interrupt your focus, note them, but bring your attention back to your breath.

Walking meditation is a good thing to try on a lunch or midday break. When you try walking meditation, you will look for a quiet place roughly twenty feet long. Then, you will walk slowly back and forth between these spots. Instead of noticing the sounds, people, and cars around you, focus on your walking. Pay attention to your subtle movements, how your body keeps balance, and be aware of how much energy it takes just for you to stand upright. This practice is good for about ten to fifteen minutes but can be shorter if you just need to get away from the desk for a few moments.

For **body scan meditation**, the best practice is to lie on your back with your arms and legs spread out to your sides. Make sure your palms are facing up. If you want to scan your body and you are at work, sitting is fine as well—you can turn your palms up in your lap if you need a few minutes to try this.

Once you are comfortable, you will close your eyes and bring all your focus to your toes. Then the pad of your foot, then your heel, and move up to your ankle, calves, knees, etc. Keep moving up your body in small increments (Mayo Clinic Staff, 2020). Make sure to touch every part of your body that you can recall and do it systematically. Essentially, you will be running a scan of your body.

Each time you touch a new area, bring your sensations, emotions, and thoughts to the forefront. Each part may incur new senses and bring about new revelations.

You can practice any of the above exercises whenever the mood strikes you or you can carve out some time to work on them. The more you use mindfulness exercises, the easier they will settle into your routine. Evidence from studies has found that anyone can benefit from engaging their senses when they are outdoors (Mayo Clinic Staff, 2020).

Trying different mindfulness exercises daily for six months will help you have an effortless transition into using the practices when you need them. You can make a commitment to nurture and reconnect with yourself and you will have an amazing set of tools to help you with ADHD symptoms, stress, and other experiences (Mayo Clinic Staff, 2020).

Conclusion

Learning how your ADHD symptoms affect your daily life will help you move toward a more organized mind, which will trickle down into everything else in your world.

The next chapter will discuss the executive function and give you an idea of how to build up better skills to develop growth and manage your ADHD a little more.

CHAPTER THREE

Executive Function & ADHD

Introduction

Being a woman with ADHD comes with a unique set of challenges that have not been fully studied yet. However, one thing that is incredibly common with ADHD is that executive function skill sets are not fully developed—up to 90% of kids who are diagnosed with ADHD also have issues with executive functions.

Executive function skills help establish structures and strategies for managing projects and determine the actions required to move each project forward (Davis & Hill, 2022). This skill set was supposed to develop fully in childhood, alongside certain fine and gross motor skills. However, when your brain has ADHD, the cognitive process that organizes your activities and thoughts, prioritizes tasks, makes decisions, and manages time efficiently does not develop correctly.

This undeveloped part of the brain happens due to an inability of your neurons to speak to one another as they would if your brain were neurotypical.

Executive Function and ADHD

Executive functions establish follow through and strategy building with projects, complete things on a deadline, and more. When there is executive dysfunction, you struggle to plan, organize, schedule, complete tasks, and analyze important things. You would also have issues keeping track of materials and prioritizing and tend to get overwhelmed by big projects (Barkley & Novotni, 2022).

If this sounds like an issue you are having with ADHD, this chapter will help you pinpoint some of the more troublesome issues and give you some tips on how to begin to build a better structure of executive skills.

Some people with ADHD have issues with executive function because these skills form in the prefrontal cortex, where most ADHD issues also occur. These neurodivergent traits happen because there is a lack of chemicals needed for the brain to communicate in a neurotypical way.

Although up to 90% of those diagnosed with ADHD have executive function issues, not everyone with executive function issues may have ADHD (at least, not that has been discovered as of the writing of this workbook).

You will be able to see the links below between executive function and the neurodivergent way your ADHD works. There are four "circuits" that connect certain parts of your brain. When these circuits do not function properly, there is a lack of communication—this creates issues with time management, goal setting, and more.

The four circuits are as follows:

The Who—this is a circuit that travels from the frontal lobe to the back hemisphere of your brain. It is where self-awareness happens, which is how you know what you are externally and internally feeling, how you know what you do, and what is happening to you.

The What—is a circuit that connects the frontal lobe to the basal ganglia, specifically, the striatum. This part of your brain is linked to memory and is attached to how we think and do. This circuit is important for plans, goals, and the future.

The Why—is a circuit that bridges the frontal lobe and the central brain, or the anterior cingulate, to the amygdala. The amygdala opens to the limbic system, which is linked to your emotions and joins together how you think and feel. In this circuit, your thoughts will invoke your feelings, and your feelings will invoke your thoughts.

The "why" circuit determines the final marker of your plans. If you think about multiple things at a time, this part of your brain will choose the option that best suits the moment, motivation, and emotional properties that match your feelings.

The When—this circuit will travel from the prefrontal area back to the cerebellum. This part of your brain is the backmost area, which coordinates the sequence of actions and the timeliness of when you get certain things done. If you have issues with time management, your "when" circuit is working improperly.

As you see the connection between synapse miscommunication and the ability of the core circuits to work together, you will see how they connect with ADHD. When these circuits miscommunicate, they will affect the main skills driven by executive function (Barkley & Novotni, 2022). These skills are described in the article "What is Executive Function? 7 Deficits Tied to ADHD" by Dr. Russell Barkely. Barkley says that the seven deficits that are tied to ADHD are:

1. **Self-awareness**—attention directed at yourself by you.

2. **Inhibition**—controlling your actions and not indulging in every thought or idea.

3. **Non-verbal working memory**—the ability to hold visual images in your mind and describe how well you can picture things.

4. **Verbal working memory**—inner dialogue.

5. **Emotional self-regulation**—using the first four executive functions to help you process and alter feelings toward specific events.

6. **Self-motivation**—motivation when there is no immediate outside consequence. How often do you finish something when you have nothing to lose or gain?

7. **Planning and problem solving**—how you play with information to come up with things, especially if there is a snag or snarl. This skill shows that there is always another way of doing things (Barkley & Novotni, 2022).

These functions should develop over time and tend to do so chronologically. In people with neurotypical brains, self-awareness develops by age two, and by age thirty, executive function skill sets should be fully formed. Those with neurodivergent brains and diagnosed with ADHD are roughly forty percent behind their peers when developing one function to the next.

Because this happens, children and adults with ADHD have had trouble dealing with relevant age situations and tend to act and think like those from a younger age bracket.

Exercise Eight: Testing your Adult Executive Function Skills

Executive dysfunction can certainly create struggles in every aspect of your life. You may have challenges completing, organizing, scheduling, and planning tasks. You may also have issues balancing tasks, recalling what needs to be done, making multi-step directions, staying on track, holding yourself accountable, and finishing tasks.

Below is a self-diagnosis test that will help you know if you have signs of executive dysfunctions—this is not a formal diagnosis. You can take this test to show your medical professional where you are and they can work out a treatment plan to strengthen your skillset.

How quickly do you let go of your anger as easily as it came on?

- Very Often
- Rarely

- Often
- Never

- Sometimes

How often do you tell yourself, "I will do it later," and then forget about it completely?

- Very Often
- Rarely

- Often
- Never

- Sometimes

How often do you become absorbed in projects that interest you to the detriment of other obligations and even people?

- Very Often
- Often
- Sometimes

- Rarely
- Never

How frequently do you forget important things, even those important to you?

- Very Often
- Often
- Sometimes

- Rarely
- Never

How quickly do you become frustrated when things do not go to plan? Does your frustration follow up with anger?

- Very Often
- Often
- Sometimes

- Rarely
- Never

How often do you become distracted by things you hear or see?

- Very Often
- Often
- Sometimes

- Rarely
- Never

Do you often lose interest in tasks quickly, even when you start with enthusiasm?

- Very Often
- Often
- Sometimes

- Rarely
- Never

How messy is your personal space? Do you frequently struggle with clutter?

- Very Often
- Often
- Sometimes
- Rarely
- Never

How difficult is it for you to move from one task to another and complete a task?

- Very Difficult
- Often Difficult
- Sometimes Difficult
- Rarely
- Never

Do you have issues knowing where to start on a project? Can you prioritize the items in a list?

- Very Often
- Often
- Sometimes
- Rarely
- Never

How frequently do you have problems starting or initiating tasks?

- Very Often
- Often
- Sometimes
- Rarely
- Never

How often do you misplace or lose items? For example, wallet, cellphone, glasses, keys, etc.?

- Very Often
- Often
- Sometimes
- Rarely
- Never

How hard is it for you to follow conversations due to distractions or remember what you wanted to say?

- Very Often
- Often
- Sometimes
- Rarely
- Never

Can you start or do things when the activity does not highly stimulate you?

- Very Often
- Often
- Sometimes
- Rarely
- Never

How often do you forget an appointment or are late for an event?

- Very Often
- Often
- Sometimes
- Rarely
- Never

Have you wasted time trying to choose what to do first in an event, activity, or project?

- Very Often
- Often
- Sometimes
- Rarely
- Never

(Bailey & Panel, 2022)

Look at your answers to the questionnaire above. Does that sound like you? Did you answer most of the questions as "sometimes, often, or very often?" Do you struggle with knowing how to help yourself and figuring out what steps to take to help build your executive function skills? The exercise below can help you with those. Also, find some simple strategies to set you on the right path.

Although there are many ways to reinforce executive function skills, below is a quick overview of strategies that can help you know where to start. Effective strategies can help you when facing challenges and will bolster your methods with healthy tools.

General Strategies

- Chunk your projects into small sub-tasks.

- Use visual organizational tools. For example, whiteboards, virtual calendars, phone notifications, etc.

- Use time organizers like watches, alarms, timers, etc.

- Ask for both written and oral directions when you are able.

- Use a visual schedule and continue to check it throughout the day (set reminders to do so).

- Plan for a time between tasks to transition from one project to another.

Manage Your Time

- Use a to-do list and estimate how long each task will take.

- Use the chunk method for all projects and assign deadlines for completing each chunk.

- Use your visual schedule to track due dates, chores, activities, and long-term projects.

- Use virtual calendars or apps to help manage your schedule and daily calendars or planners to write the same information.

- Tag each assignment with a deadline (no matter how small it seems).

Space and Material

- Purchase decorative and colorful organizers to clean up your workspace.

- Keep important objects that you will use daily or weekly in your line of view or clear containers so you will not forget about them.

- Put anything away that you will not or have not used in the last month. Add them to storage containers with lids.

- Throw away any clutter that is not a bill or important piece of paper. Clear your desk of everything but a few tools.

- Separate workspaces. Keep work stuff in one area, bills in another, etc.

- Schedule a time to organize and clean your workspace each week.

At work

- Create a checklist for assignments.

- Put the due date on the project.

- Reread directions.

- Follow up with my manager.

- Troubleshoot problems.

- List any new issues.

- Close out the project for the day.

(LD Online Writing Staff, n.d.)

While some of these items may sound as though they are simple or even maybe repetitive to what you have heard in the past, do not knock them until you try them. If you have tried them already, try them one more time. You do not know what will stick with you now as opposed to what place you were in previously.

Although you do have to find the right strategy for how your mind works and how your habits will form, make sure to try processes for 21 days or longer before you give up doing them. Also, remember that things will be easier to do at first, then will feel more difficult, and you will want to quit, but keep moving. Dig your heels in if you have to, you are worth putting in the effort for. You deserve to live a life with a little less clutter and chaos. And the methods above may just be a gateway for doing them.

Exercise Nine: Practice Builds Skills

Executive function skills are a mental toolkit for success (Hendry et al., 2016). And although Hendry and his colleagues discussed the idea of toddlers developing these skills, if your executive functions are latent or were not developed, you incur more frustration than you need. While executive function is predictive of career or academic success, know that it has nothing to do with how smart you are (Alloway & Alloway, 2010).

Building these skills will not take much more than a little determination and commitment. Also, note that the less you impair your executive functions with things like stress or strain, you will be able to help them flourish, which is another reason to be kind to yourself (Diamond, 2022).

The activities below will focus on three core executive functions. These skills will be

1. Inhibitory Control.

2. Working Memory.

3. Cognitive Flexibility.

Inhibitory control can be seen in examples like resisting temptations, curbing impulsivity, and thinking before taking action or speaking. Situations like staying on task no matter how bored you are require inhibitory control

Some activities that can help you improve inhibitory control are below:

- Play Simon Says—it sounds silly and can be, but when you have a friend, partner, or child, be Simon and follow their instructions. You can have a great time while building up some new skills.

- Go to an acting class. Perform comedy or drama scenes to build inhibitions through other characters.

- Play music with other people in your house. Everyone gets to listen to one song, and you must wait your turn to do it.

- Tag team listening. Take turns with a partner or friend by reading something or listening to the other person read. This practice will strengthen your communication skills by having to listen instead of speaking over others (Diamond, 2022).

- Listen to stories. Using audiobooks as tools will allow you to concentrate on what is being said without visual aids. Sustained auditory attention with a story will strengthen your focus and attention control.

- Learning balance. Balance is all about focusing on one thing to meet a specific goal. Some balanced activities can be:

  - *Walking on any line*—this can be straight or curved. If you find that it is too easy to follow the line, put something in your hand or on your head to level the task up.

  - *Use a bell when you walk*—hold a bell and walk without making a noise. This activity is good to use when you need to calm down.

  - *Find a log*—just like walking on a line, using a log will force focus, or you will fall. Be careful not to hurt yourself, and do not walk on a log over a gorge or high from the ground. Keep your logs to ones that have already fallen and are fully grounded.

- Use crafts to build concentration and reduce clumsiness. Beading or braiding work well for both of these.

When using **working memory**, your brain will absorb and hold information in your mind. It will then process the information to play or work with it. If your mind does not manipulate it that way, the data will be stored in short-term memory and quickly forgotten.

Although both are important, working memory and short-term memory use information differently. Working memory will allow you to:

- Engage in self-reflection.

- Consider the future.

- Reflect on past instances.

- Mentally play with ideas and relate them to others.

- Use multi-layered instructions and follow them in the order they are supposed to go in.

- Remember the questions you want to ask during conversations as they are happening.

- Make sense of events and occurrences that happen over time.

Activities that will improve your working memory can be:

- Use your math skills. Calculate discounts, tips, and totals while shopping. Do this in your mind to strengthen your working memory.

- Sit in a group or at a party and play a storytelling game. One person starts the story, the next person repeats what is said and adds a little more to the story, and the story continues until everyone has repeated and added to the story.

- Listen to audiobooks. Whereas inhibitory practices will develop in a specific way with audiobooks, when you use them, you are also improving your working memory by ingesting and absorbing details where you can relate to new information.

    - Perform poetry or slam poetry out loud. This will have you memorizing short bursts of words and build your attention. As a side note, you do not have to perform the poetry in front of anyone, just say the poems aloud and build on your memory skills (Diamond, 2022).

Cognitive flexibility includes the ability to:

- Think outside the box.

- See other people's perspectives.

- Take a chance on a sudden opportunity.

- Find success despite challenges or barriers.

- Adjust to unexpected issues that occur.

- Admit you were wrong after you hear new information.

If you are looking for activities to improve your cognitive flexibility, try some of the ideas below:

- Improvise. Participate in theater programs and music lessons that encourage creativity with a need to adjust quickly. Some examples can be jazz and dance.

- Use out-of-the-box objects. Come up with unique uses for everyday objects. For example, use your kitchen table for something else other than eating. Could it be a fort? A drum? What else? Pens can be used to write, but they can also hold hair up in a bun, clean out tight spots, and other things.

- Look for common items. Find common traits between daily items. How are carrots and cucumbers similar? How is your car like a foot? Come up with a list of daily items and find out how they can connect.

- Solve real-life problems. As typical as this exercise sounds, solving everyday problems is part of your daily routine, even if it is not in your job description. When you come across a problem, do you try to troubleshoot until you resolve it, or do you pass it off to someone else because you "cannot" do something? Instead of pulling the trigger and handing the problem to someone else, try to solve the problem yourself unless you find that someone will get hurt because of it.

If none of the items above sound interesting, you can find other places to improve your executive function skills in the activities below:

- Learn how to cook and bake.

- Find creative outlets like crafting or painting.

- Caring for animals, children, the elderly, etc.

- Engage in the arts like theater, dance, or music

- Join a league or sports team.

- Participate in martial arts.

- Learn how to survive in the wild.

- Practice woodworking.

The activities above involve planning, perseverance, creative problem-solving, and cognitive flexibility, which marries all the executive function skills together.

Executive functions are also a precursor to stress and self-esteem. When your stress levels are high and your self-esteem is low, your executive function skills may seem as though they are on the fritz. Below are some methods to help lower your stress levels and build your self-image. Try them out and see what works best for you.

- **Ask for help**. You cannot do everything on your own, despite what society says you have to or should do. It is wrong to assume that you must "do it all." Instead, find strength by reaching out for help and getting advice, guidance, and information you would not have known otherwise. It may bruise your ego, but once you are in a good role with it, you will see how incredible it can be.

- **Build a stable routine**. Find predictability, clarity, and consistency with what you will and will not accept in your daily life. This process can take a little work but will help you reduce stress and build confidence by creating healthy boundaries at work, at home, and with friends.

- **Understand that mistakes are part of the learning process**. Making a mistake is not a bad thing. It is an opportunity to stretch your current abilities and to help you learn something new. Having a growth mindset will build your confidence and give you a chance to rewrite the directive you have on how to treat yourself when errors occur.

- **Get a pet**. Even though a huge responsibility comes with owning a pet, these fuzzy little guys will help improve your mood and reduce stress (Barker et al., 38; Gee et al., 230; R. T. Barker et al. 29).

- **Find self-compassion.** When you learn how to be kind to yourself despite the mistakes you make and the flaws you have, you begin to teach yourself that being perfect is not the goal to strive for. Also, compassion for yourself leads to compassion for others, so you are helping out more people than you realize.

- **Exercise**. Getting into a moving action will relieve much stress. Also, activities where you burn energy, encourage healthy sleep habits, release more chemicals in your brain, and will keep you in a healthier state of mind.

- **Be mindful**. When you move and think with mindful intentions, you are allowing yourself to build up every part of executive functionality and granting yourself a reprieve from your ADHD symptoms. Daily mindfulness will make you aware of your actions and thoughts before they happen and will give you the chance to forgive yourself when you respond in a different way than you wanted to (Diamond, 2022).

Exercise Ten: Self-Reflection of Executive Function Skills

Now that you have read up on executive function skills and know where it connects with you, you can think about different times in your day when executive dysfunction may slide into place over the functionality. Make a list below in each section to see your issues with time management, organization, planning, problem-solving, self-awareness, and more.

Once you discover where your pain points are, you can develop goals and create a plan to move forward on strengthening your skills.

Where do I have issues with Time Management?

For example, I am rarely on time

_____

_____

_____

_____

_____

_____

_____

_____

_____

_____

_____

_____

_____

_____

_____

_____

_____

_____

_____

_____

Where do I have planning issues?

For example, I can never plan to go to the grocery store, even though I mean to do it.

_____

_____

_____

_____

_____

_____

_____

_____

_____

_____

_____

_____

_____

_____

_____

_____

_____

What do I have trouble remembering?

For example, I usually forget about my children's performances, events, and meetings until the day I have to scramble around to make everything work.

_____

_____

_____

_____

_____

_____

_____

_____

_____

_____

_____

_____

_____

_____

_____

_____

How quickly do I get angry?

_____
_____
_____
_____
_____
_____
_____
_____
_____
_____
_____
_____
_____

How often do I get absorbed in a project because it is so interesting? What kind of activities, events, and people do I forget because of it?

For example, I recently discovered Jam Making. I became obsessed, bought all the tools and supplies needed, forgot to pick up my daughter from school one day, and let the laundry pile up to the point that I was overwhelmed and did not want to do it.

_____
_____
_____
_____
_____
_____
_____
_____
_____
_____
_____
_____

How often do I get interested in a subject and become so hyperfocused initially, and when the thrill dies away, I leave the project where it is and never finish it?

For instance, I really enjoy knitting. I knit so much that I decide I want to sell my wares. Halfway through setting up an Etsy store, it becomes too frustrating, I get too tired, and then I have never gotten around to selling them.

_____
_____
_____
_____
_____
_____
_____
_____
_____
_____
_____

You can create more lists and categories based on other information in this chapter. When you write things down, you'll have an amazing opportunity to see the thoughts in your head and build a better form of self-reflection.

Once you have the list created above and can see where your main trigger points are, you can begin to build goals for where you want to be and how you want to strengthen your executive function skill set. See the next exercise and map out some of your goals.

Exercise Eleven: Goals for Building Executive Function Skills

You can build your executive function skills by planning out how to build executive function skills. You are probably right if that sentence seems redundant, but the sentiment is not. Like in the previous section, where you read about solving daily, real-life problems, this exercise allows you to do just that by mapping out goals, breaking them into chunks, setting deadlines, and building skills that can improve your life's structure. See the example below and follow the breadcrumbs to build a goal and deadline that works for you.

Example goal map:

Goal: I want to remember people's names more often.

Deadline: Three months.

Step (Chunk) One: When I meet a new person, repeat their name. For example, "Hello, Shirley, it is nice to meet you." And "I hope you have a nice day, Shirley." When they walk away, repeat their name to yourself one last time.

Deadline: One month. Meet new people by asking individuals for help. You can ask sales representatives for their names at stores, gas stations, etc.

Step (Chunk) Two: When you see them again, ask them what their name is. You can politely say, "Excuse me, can you tell me your name again?" That way, you can remind yourself if you are right, wrong, or forgotten.

Deadline: The next time you see this person.

Step (Chunk) Three: Call them by their name each time you see them.

Deadline: any time after your second encounter. Do not be afraid to ask them for their name again if you forget.

Notes: Once you get into the habit of remembering people's names, you will not be able to say that you are no longer good with names. Instead, you will find that you remember most people's names more often than not.

Your Turn: Try three goals to build executive function skills

Goal One:

_____

_____

_____

_____

_____

_____

Deadline:

_____

_____

_____

_____

Step (Chunk) One:

_____

_____

_____

_____

Deadline:

_____

_____

_____

_____

Step (Chunk) Two:

_____

_____

_____

_____

Deadline:

_____

_____

_____

_____

Step (Chunk) Three:

_____

_____

_____

_____

Deadline:

_____

_____

_____

_____

Notes:

_____

_____

_____

_____

_____

_____

_____

_____

_____

_____

_____

_____

_____

_____

_____

_____

_____

Goal Two:

_____

_____

_____

_____

_____

Deadline:

_____

_____

_____

_____

_____

Step (Chunk) One:

_____

_____

_____

_____

Deadline:

_____

_____

_____

_____

Step (Chunk) Two:

_____

_____

_____

_____

_____

Deadline:

_____
_____
_____
_____

Step (Chunk) Three:

_____
_____
_____
_____

Deadline:

_____
_____
_____
_____

Notes:

_____
_____
_____
_____
_____
_____
_____
_____
_____
_____

Goal Three:

_____

_____

_____

_____

_____

Deadline:

_____

_____

_____

_____

_____

Step (Chunk) One:

_____

_____

_____

_____

Deadline:

_____

_____

_____

_____

Step (Chunk) Two:

_____

_____

_____

_____

_____

Deadline:

_____

_____

_____

_____

Step (Chunk) Three:

_____

_____

_____

_____

Deadline:

_____

_____

_____

_____

Notes:

_____

_____

_____

_____

_____

_____

_____

_____

_____

_____

_____

Once you build your three goals, incorporate one of them into your schedule or routine at a time to avoid getting overwhelmed by new practices. When you find that your interest is waning, make sure to keep going with the project. This part is where you must develop some determination and commitment with self-awareness.

Completing goals will help build confidence in yourself and give you the resolution with executive function.

Conclusion

With the development of any latent executive function skills, you will build self-confidence and feel you can manage life a little better. You will have a plan where you can implement new goals and create new milestones to climb. The more you do this practice, the more it will infuse into your daily life until the method becomes automatic whenever you have a goal or plan you want to tackle.

In the next chapter, you will learn about emotional regulation and rejection sensitivity.

CHAPTER FOUR

Emotional Regulation & Rejection Sensitivity

Introduction

There are times when our emotions get out of hand. There are other times when we are perfectly fine. And yet there are a few times when our emotions feel like they will blow a circuit.

In this seemingly never-ending cycle of emotional ups and downs, it cannot be easy to find kindness for yourself, especially if you have been labeled with one of those tags that assertive, emotive, and expressive women some (most) times receive. The "overly emotional," "crybaby," "insane," etc. are names that do not reflect who you are as a person but follow you around like a black cloud nonetheless.

First, you should know that emotional dysregulation is a huge symptom for women dealing with ADHD. Emotional dysregulation is caused by a lack of chemicals released in your brain to make it function like a neurotypical brain. When this happens, it becomes harder to control where, when, why, and how your emotions implode.

While this is not your fault, you can work on managing it to the point where it will barely seem like a blip on your radar.

This chapter will discuss emotional regulation and rejection sensitivity.

These two topics go hand in hand. The more rejection you felt as a child, the less you can regulate your emotions. The rejection you had when you were a child may have been real, or it may have been a perception of your insecurity. Rejection Sensitivity Dysphoria (RSD) connects with your womanhood, ADHD, and feelings in a way that may blow up your day when you feel attached.

In the book Women with ADHD, we shared a sentiment with our readers. This sentiment still holds today. Please see it below.

"If you have issues with emotional regulation, we hope that by reading this information, you will find relief and know that you are affected not because of your personality but by how your brain developed. Understand that RSD can be managed by introducing healthy coping mechanisms into your daily life (Davis & Hill, 2022)."

What is Emotional Regulation?

Anyone with ADHD can have issues with regulating their emotions. If you feel as though your feelings are on a rollercoaster and you are unsure of what will happen at any given time, you can become confused, bewildered, and befuddled by your emotions and how they react when something doesn't happen the way you anticipate it should.

Emotional regulation is the opposite of dysregulation.

When you are emotionally deregulated, you have an impaired ability to control emotional responses when in certain situations. This dysregulation leads to overblown and extreme reactions that will not fit the circumstances. Some of the symptoms are:

- Reactions that seem out of sync with what happened.

- You cannot calm down, even when aware of your overreaction.

- Become frustrated or annoyed easily—have a low tolerance for this.

- Getting overwhelmed by your emotions.

- Prone to sudden outbursts or are increasingly temperamental.

- Having a difficult time calming down.

When your emotions are deregulated, you will feel like you go from zero to 100 in the blink of an eye. Triggers can be all around you and seemingly random, and you can get frustrated because your preferred yogurt is sold out at the grocery store or you did not get the promotion at work. Do not let your disappointment grow overwhelming.

The key is to separate your emotions from reality. Eventually, you can ask yourself: How important is this? What is a rational response to the disappointing situation?

However, first, you must recognize your emotional dysregulation and see how it affects every element of your life.

Emotional dysregulation can be the most disruptive part of ADHD.

The inability to moderate your response in any environment, like work, home, or socially, can change how people, co-workers, friends, and family members view and interact with you. If you have a temperamental or hypersensitive label at work, you may suffer for it, promotion-wise. You may also put too much undue stress on yourself and focus on the small details instead of looking at the bigger picture.

With personal and romantic relationships, minor issues can become a full blow until your partner, friends, and family may distance themselves from you because they no longer wish to walk on eggshells.

This emotional imbalance can also lead to low self-esteem, self-doubt, and uncertainty about what to do when something arises. Reacting as though every hurdle is catastrophic can become physically and mentally exhausting. There may be times when you just feel as though you want to give up (Green and Colemen, 2022).

Emotional dysregulation is a common symptom of ADHD, although it is rarely discussed. Science has shown that there are too many causes of emotional dysregulation with ADHD. These include an overactive amygdala and an underactive frontal cortex (Shaw et al., 2014).

Your amygdala triggers emotional responses, so when one is overactive, your emotional responses to smaller issues may be much bigger than they need to be. Then, your frontal cortex inhibits and filters emotions so you can react accordingly.

However, when your frontal cortex underreacts, you will have latent responses to controlling your emotions. Combining these two factors will lead to impulsivity, hypersensitivity, and explosions.

You will find five dimensions of a neurotypical brain and how they work with emotional regulation. These levels are listed below:

1. Recognize your emotions

2. Recognize emotions in others.

3. Emotional Reactivity—what is your threshold, how intense are your emotions, and how long do these emotions last?

4. How to reduce your aroused emotions.

5. How to improve your mood and generate better emotions (Green and Colemen, 2022).

Women with ADHD struggle the most with number three. Suppose you consider that your amygdala is overreacting and generates tense feelings that can push the emotional threshold to the limit more often and quickly.

Exercise Twelve: How Are My Emotions Dysregulated?

For this exercise, you will need to become more aware of your emotions and how you react. Even if you think you were justified with your reaction, you need to address the situation from a more objective standpoint and look at different perspectives.

Instructions:

- Write down an instance where you emotionally blew up.

- Examine your reaction. Ask yourself:

    ○ What happened?

    ○ What triggered your reaction?

- ○ How did it feel when you were reacting?

- ○ Could you have reacted differently?

- How did the other person respond?

- When you answer these questions, be honest and objective. Do this three times for exercise twelve, but continue to look at your emotional reactions and reflect on how they could be approached differently and if the situation really needed such a big reaction.

- **Emotional Reaction One:**

_____

_____

_____

_____

_____

What happened?

_____

_____

_____

_____

What triggered your reaction?

_____

_____

_____

_____

_____

How did it feel when you were reacting?

_____

_____

_____

_____

_____

Could you have reacted differently?

_____

_____

_____

_____

_____

How did the other person respond?

_____

_____

_____

_____

_____

- **Emotional Reaction Two:**

_____

_____

_____

_____

What happened?

_____

_____

_____

_____

What triggered your reaction?

_____

_____

_____

_____

How did it feel when you were reacting?

_____

_____

_____

_____

Could you have reacted differently?

_____

_____

_____

_____

How did the other person respond?

_____

_____

_____

_____

- **Emotional Reaction Three**:

_____

_____

_____

_____

What happened?

_____

_____

_____

_____

What triggered your reaction?

_____

_____

_____

_____

How did it feel when you were reacting?

_____

_____

_____

_____

Could you have reacted differently?

_____

_____

_____

_____

How did the other person respond?

_____

_____

_____

_____

Once you have filled out three instances, do not stop with your self-reflection. Instead, use this exercise to spur new examinations each time you react in a way that seems over the top. While you can use self-reflection and self-awareness tools to observe your reactions, try some of the strategies below. These methods can help you build a better routine when your emotions rise.

- **Name your emotions**. If you are feeling angry, frustrated, happy, giddy, etc., and it seems overblown, name the emotion you are feeling. Then, redirect yourself differently before you react. You can try some of the following ideas to see if they help distract you from the big emotion:

  ○ Leave. Move from whatever room you are in and leave the situation. Stand in the backyard, get a drink of water, go for a walk, or more. If you have another person involved, tell them you need to take a few minutes so you can catch your breath and process your feelings.

  ○ Be aware of what your body is doing. Are you sweating? Do you find it hard to breathe? Can you feel your heart race?

  ○ Describe the feeling you have named. Be as specific as possible. You can write about this, talk it out with another person, or just say the information out loud and to an empty room.

- **Make an emotional journal**. Getting your emotions out onto the paper gets them out of your head and heart. If you can pour them out of yourself without physical, mental, and emotional harm to anyone, you may feel some relief. This process is an active way of expressing yourself, even if no one else hears it.

- **Exercise**. Women with ADHD struggle to disengage their emotions from their thoughts and actions. If you find that you cannot calm down, go work out. Exerting physical energy can use up excessive stress and burn off that overblown feeling. This energy depletion can help you avoid yelling and screaming and can help you sort through the real problem.

- **Use music**. You can play an instrument or listen to music. When you do this, your mood will improve.

- **Make a list of coping mechanisms**. Like journaling your emotions, getting a list of coping mechanisms in front of you can get the ideas out of your head and give you a sense of accomplishment. Developing a list of coping tools will be proactive instead of reactive, which is training your brain and body to behave when other items come to pass (Green and Colemen, 2022).

- **Try ADHD medication**. While this method can be controversial, when you use medication, you are helping your brain work by filling it up with the chemicals and hormones it needs. Medicine (especially in the present) will not change who you are, what you do, how you feel, what you say, or how you think. It can help you an incredible amount, and you will be able to breathe easier. However, if you are not comfortable taking medication for any reason, you do not have to do it. Follow your gut here. You may be scared to take meds, but know it is the right choice, or you may understand that you are not ready to take that step. Either one is okay.

- **Be mindful.** Hey! Here is the buzzword "mindful" again. This time it is about emotional regulation. Mindfulness works on many levels. Incorporating mindfulness meditation into your daily life will encourage self-awareness and build a desire for growth (Bertin, 2022).

When you understand how your emotions work and how you can help regulate them, you will also see and feel your sensitivity to rejection dwindle.

What is Rejection Sensitivity?

Rejection sensitivity dysphoria (RSD) manifests emotional regulation and seriously disrupts a woman's life. If you have ADHD and have not been diagnosed until adulthood, you may have formed these symptoms over the years due to fear of rejection. Dysphoria comes into play because although you were not traumatized by rejection, you begin to see, feel, and hear rejection even with the most constructive critiques.

Women with ADHD have often described RSD as an open wound. And when they face rejection (real or dysmorphic), they will be overcome by intense pain that sometimes exposes them to extreme emotional reactions. If you have RSD with your ADHD, you have developed this disorder because you have never found healthy or effective ways to cope with your symptoms or the pain of rejection (Davis & Hill, 2022).

Rejection can be an enormous trigger point for you. Your sensitivity to rejection, whether real or perceived, can make different interactions a source of pain. Even when you feel there is a possibility of rejection, you can begin to avoid many things. When you avoid potential rejection, you can stop yourself from trying new things, taking chances in your career, and even being fearful of breaking away from chaos (Dodson & Saline, 2022).

Our book Women with ADHD rejects sensitivity at length and how it can even elicit shame and cause a more open willingness to engage in sexual activities because sex equals social acceptance.

"You [may] have already taken part in risky sexual behavior or have thought about it often. You may have also had younger initiations into intercourse and other sexual activity, more casual sex, more sexual partners, and less protected sex with more transmissible sexual infections. You may have even had more unplanned pregnancies because of unsafe sexual practices (Davis & Hill, 2022; Dodson & Saline, 2022)."

Of course, rejection sensitivity is more than just having too many sexual encounters or fear of trying new things. Dr. William Dodson LF-APA writes for *ADDitude* online frequently. In his article, "How ADHD Ignites Rejection Sensitive Dysphoria (2022)," Dodson writes:

"Rejection sensitive dysphoria is one manifestation of emotional dysregulation, a common but misunderstood and under-researched symptom of ADHD in adults. Individuals with RSD feel 'unbearable' pain as a result of perceived or actual rejection, teasing, or criticism that is not alleviated with cognitive or dialectical behavior therapy."

What Dodson is explaining is the pain and anxiety that comes from even an idea of rejection—this happens when someone experiences brain-based symptoms that are traumatic but not caused by trauma when it comes to rejection. While it is not a formal diagnosis of ADHD, it is pegged as a "disruptive manifestation of emotional dysregulation—a common, but under-researched and misunderstood symptom of

ADHD, particularly in adults (2022)."

One-third of adult patients with ADHD report that they have RSD and that it is the most paralyzing part of their disorder because they cannot find ways to cope or manage the pain RSD can cause.

Rejection Sensitive Dysphoria can be caused by rejection, teasing, criticism, and negative self–talk prompted by contrived or real failures. It is characterized by "intense mood shifts triggered by distinct episodes following the previous causes (Dodson, 2022).

Review some of the outward signs of RSD to see if any of them sound familiar:

- Emotional outbursts that follow criticism or rejection, whether real or contrived.

- Avoidance of social situations.

- Thoughts of self-harm or negative self-talk.

- Poor perception of self or low self-esteem.

- Negative and continuous self-talk can be seen as "being your own worst enemy."

- Recurring and ruminating thoughts.

- Problems with relationships, constantly feeling rejected or defensive.

Although there is always a slight change in misdiagnosis, understanding the difference between a mood disorder, like social anxiety, and RSD with ADHD can help determine if you should pursue other options.

If you have a mood disorder, your symptoms will look more like the following:

- Untriggered mood changes (often seemingly out of the blue).

- Moods are not reflective of what is going on in our life.

- There is a gradual shift in your mood over the weeks.

- The offset of your mood will last weeks to months.

- The duration of mood shift is two weeks or longer (Dodson, 2022).

For RSD with ADHD, your symptoms will look more like this:

- A clear trigger will shift your mood.

- Your mood will match your perception of the trigger.

- Your mood shift will be instant.

- Your mood will shift back to "normal" within hours.

While RSD is not currently paired with ADHD in the DSM–5–TR—meaning it is not a formal symptom of ADHD in the United States—in the European Union, it is one of the six fundamental features of an ADHD diagnosis. And while there is a big push to include RSD in an official ADHD diagnosis, there may be reasons why it may never happen:

- RSD episodes are not always present.

- It comes in triggered bursts and is hard to measure.

- Those with RSD are usually ashamed of their over-reactions and hide them to avoid being labeled mentally unstable or overly emotional (Dodson, 2022).

Rejection sensitivity dysphoria is a serious issue that can be managed and even turned around with help through talk therapy and a behavioral treatment plan. Dodson claims that "[RSD] is difficult for people with ADHD to describe, but all who have it agree that it feels awful. Indeed, the term dysphoria is literally Greek for 'unbearable (2002).'"

You may not have RSD, you may secretly see some of the symptoms in your actions, or you may suspect that you have this part of ADHD. Take the quiz below to give yourself a better idea about it. The quiz is not meant to diagnose you with RSD. This quiz is manifested in Dr. William Dodson's work and is meant for personal use that will help you discover whether a clinical evaluation is needed.

Exercise Thirteen: Do You Have Rejection Sensitivity?

Instructions: Circle the one that resonates most with your actions, thoughts, behaviors, and emotions.

When your feelings are hurt, do you experience intense bouts of rage?

- Very Often
- Often
- Sometimes
- Rarely
- Never

When you feel that you have been criticized or rejected, do you experience extreme bouts of sadness?

- Very Often
- Often
- Sometimes
- Rarely
- Never

Do you judge yourself harder than you judge others?

- Very Often
- Often
- Sometimes
- Rarely
- Never

Do you assume no one likes you, so you avoid social situations, or assume you will have anxiety no matter what?

- Very Often
- Often
- Sometimes
- Rarely
- Never

Do you see yourself going above and beyond to get on someone's good side? Do you consider yourself a people pleaser?

- Very Often
- Often
- Sometimes
- Rarely
- Never

Do you pass on opportunities at work or home because you are afraid you will fail (or not complete them)?

- Very Often
- Often
- Sometimes
- Rarely
- Never

Has anyone called you "overly sensitive," "overly emotional," "a head case," etc., due to your strong emotional reactions?

- Very Often
- Often
- Sometimes
- Rarely
- Never

Do you often feel pressured to be "perfect" to avoid making mistakes and thereby getting rejected or a bad critique?

- Very Often
- Often
- Sometimes
- Rarely
- Never

Do you experience physical emotions, like you have been punched in the chest or physically "wounded?"

- Very Often
- Often
- Sometimes
- Rarely
- Never

Are you often ashamed of how you cannot seem to control your emotions?

- Very Often
- Often
- Sometimes
- Rarely
- Never

Have you been told you had a mood or borderline character disorder before you were diagnosed with ADHD?

- Very Often
- Often
- Sometimes
- Rarely
- Never

Is it easier to evade intimate relationships with friends or romantically? Are you worried that they will not like the "real you" if they get too close?

- Very Often
- Often
- Sometimes
- Rarely
- Never

Do you constantly fear that you will be fired every time your boss calls you into their office? Do you assume that commonplace interactions will always end up terribly?

- Very Often
- Rarely
- Often
- Never
- Sometimes

Do you believe that you cannot continue feeling the way you do?

- Very Often
- Rarely
- Often
- Never
- Sometimes

Do you avoid going to new places, trying new things, or meeting new people, because you fear failure, rejection, or criticism?

- Very Often
- Rarely
- Often
- Never
- Sometimes

(Dodson, 2022)

Once you fill out the questionnaire above, take some time to reflect on it. If you have answered sometimes, often, or very often more questions than not, that could be an indicator of RSD. However, you will not know for sure until you get a formal diagnosis from a clinical evaluation.

Suppose you have received a clinical evaluation and formal diagnosis. In this case, you may find that you and your mental health provider have developed a plan to divert RSD into something healthier for you to manage.

If you and your medical health professional have begun developing a behavioral treatment plan, which may or may not include medicine, you may develop mindfulness activities. Mindfulness activities will allow you to be in the moment of your emotions and thoughts, but instead of connecting to them, you will observe them from an objective position.

You can start with the exercise below that will help you start to reframe the ruminating self-deprecating thoughts and have you redirect your negative, intense emotions into a more positive way.

The exercise below will help you reframe negative thoughts and redirect uncomfortable emotions into a more positive overview.

Exercise Fourteen: How to Redirect RSD to Positivity

This activity will have you taking an objective stance on many of your more unpleasant emotions, thoughts, and feelings regarding RSD. You can begin by thinking about five to eight examples of when your RSD got the better of you. Then, you can map out the trigger, your emotions, your actions, and your calming moment. Afterward, you can reflect on how you could have handled the situation differently.

RSD is part of how your brain behaves. It may take some time to see a shift in your behavior, but with practice and persistence, you will be able to catch yourself before you have an RST reaction. You may even get to the point where you see a potential trigger and extinguish it before you get an opportunity to feel rejected without having to avoid circumstances, people, or experiences.

Instructions:

1. Think of a time when your RSD was triggered.

2. Explain what happened without giving in to the extreme emotions connected to the memory and without judging yourself, your actions, or your emotions.

3. Map out the trigger point, your actions, and how you felt about it.

4. Do you see moments where you could have done things differently?

This practice is one of mindfulness. Any insight into your behavior can prepare you for the next time things happen.

Memory One:

What happened?

_____

_____

_____

_____

What was the trigger?

_____

_____

_____

_____

_____

What did you feel?

_____

_____

_____

_____

What were your actions?

_____

_____

_____

_____

_____

What could you have done differently?

_____

_____

_____

_____

Memory Two:

What happened?

_____

_____

_____

_____

What was the trigger?

_____

_____

_____

_____

What did you feel?

_____

_____

_____

_____

What were your actions?

_____

_____

_____

What could you have done differently?

_____

_____

_____

_____

Memory Three:

What happened?

_____

_____

_____

_____

What was the trigger?

_____

_____

_____

_____

What did you feel?

_____

_____

_____

_____

What were your actions?

_____

_____

_____

What could you have done differently?

_____

_____

_____

_____

Memory Four:

What happened?

_____

_____

_____

_____

What was the trigger?

_____

_____

_____

_____

What did you feel?

_____

_____

_____

_____

What were your actions?

_____

_____

_____

What could you have done differently?

_____

_____

_____

_____

Memory Five:

What happened?

_____

_____

_____

_____

What was the trigger?

_____

_____

_____

_____

What did you feel?

_____

_____

_____

_____

What were your actions?

_____

_____

_____

What could you have done differently?

_____

_____

_____

_____

Memory Six:

What happened?

_____

_____

_____

_____

What was the trigger?

_____

_____

_____

_____

What did you feel?

_____

_____

_____

_____

What were your actions?

_____

_____

_____

_____

What could you have done differently?

_____

_____

_____

_____

Memory Seven:

What happened?

_____

_____

_____

_____

What was the trigger?

_____

_____

_____

_____

What did you feel?

_____

_____

_____

_____

What were your actions?

_____

_____

_____

What could you have done differently?

_____

_____

_____

_____

Memory Eight:

What happened?

_____

_____

_____

_____

What was the trigger?

_____

_____

_____

_____

What did you feel?

_____

_____

_____

_____

What were your actions?

_____

_____

_____

What could you have done differently?

_____

_____

_____

_____

Just because you feel rejection does not mean that rejection is the intent of the other person. Your RSD will give you an overinflated sense of negative criticism when it is more about how your brain behaves.

Exercise Fifteen: RSD Mirror—Finding Out Where You're Sensitive

Once you begin pinning the negative self-talk in your mind and you can recognize what you are saying to yourself, you can find out just where your triggers are. Use the trigger points above to see where things are sensitive. Ask yourself the following questions:

- What is the trigger?

- Why is this a trigger for me?

- Do I remember the moment or feeling of the trigger?

- Where have I been triggered like this in the past?

Use this exercise to mirror yourself and pull out some introspective thoughts. You may have a difficult time touching these emotions, and they may feel rawer than what you are expecting, so it is always important, if you have a negative reaction at first, to talk with your therapist about these things. If you feel more comfortable working through this exercise with your therapist, at least at the beginning, that is also perfectly acceptable. That idea will be applauded.

Memory One

_____

_____

_____

What is the trigger?

_____
_____
_____
_____

Why is this a trigger for me?

_____
_____
_____
_____

Do I remember the moment or feeling of the trigger?

_____
_____
_____
_____

Where have I been triggered like this in the past?

_____
_____
_____
_____
_____

Memory Two

_____
_____
_____
_____

What is the trigger?

_____

_____

_____

_____

Why is this a trigger for me?

_____

_____

_____

_____

Do I remember the moment or feeling of the trigger?

_____

_____

_____

_____

Where have I been triggered like this in the past?

_____

_____

_____

_____

Memory Three

_____

_____

_____

_____

_____

What is the trigger?

_____

_____

_____

_____

Why is this a trigger for me?

_____

_____

_____

_____

Do I remember the moment or feeling of the trigger?

_____

_____

_____

_____

Where have I been triggered like this in the past?

_____

_____

_____

_____

_____

Memory Four

_____

_____

_____

_____

What is the trigger?

_____

_____

_____

_____

Why is this a trigger for me?

_____

_____

_____

_____

Do I remember the moment or feeling of the trigger?

_____

_____

_____

_____

Where have I been triggered like this in the past?

_____

_____

_____

_____

Memory Five

_____

_____

_____

_____

What is the trigger?

_____

_____

_____

_____

Why is this a trigger for me?

_____

_____

_____

_____

Do I remember the moment or feeling of the trigger?

_____

_____

_____

_____

Where have I been triggered like this in the past?

_____

_____

_____

_____

Memory Six

_____

_____

_____

_____

What is the trigger?

_____

_____

_____

_____

Why is this a trigger for me?

_____

_____

_____

_____

Do I remember the moment or feeling of the trigger?

_____

_____

_____

_____

Where have I been triggered like this in the past?

_____

_____

_____

_____

Memory Seven

_____

_____

_____

_____

What is the trigger?

_____

_____

_____

_____

Why is this a trigger for me?

_____

_____

_____

_____

Do I remember the moment or feeling of the trigger?

_____

_____

_____

_____

Where have I been triggered like this in the past?

_____

_____

_____

_____

Memory Eight

_____

_____

_____

_____

What is the trigger?

_____
_____
_____
_____

Why is this a trigger for me?

_____
_____
_____
_____

Do I remember the moment or feeling of the trigger?

_____
_____
_____
_____

Where have I been triggered like this in the past?

_____
_____
_____
_____

Acceptance—Break The Silence And Take Center Stage

By the time you are an adult, you have learned to hide your ADHD symptoms, especially if you have had to conform to certain ideas of what a woman, wife, mom, etc., should be like. You may just be trying to fit in and be "normal." Alternatively, you may have rejected the entire idea of societal norms and are living a different kind of life.

No matter your approach to your ADHD-ness, you will still have to accept that part of yourself. Just as you have learned to accept, your hormones will be in flux, and anytime you get on a phone call, your child will need you as if it is the most important thing in the entire world (if you are a mother).

Problems occur if you do not begin to accept the issues that ADHD can bring into your life. Two of the most common occurrences are low self-esteem and self-harm. Most women struggle with their internalized sense of impairments, which affects their sense of self and how they manage their life skills.

Many women even believe they are not entitled to a support system because they are where everyone else comes to get support, which could not be further from the truth.

You may also blame yourself for being too distracted to catch up on daily responsibilities. You may allow your disorganization, lateness, and lack of motivation to be an excuse for people to reject or criticize you. You may begin censoring yourself.

When your premenstrual hormone levels fluctuate, you can experience various ADHD symptoms, such as higher rates of irritability, negative moods, sleep issues, and trouble focusing. These symptoms can easily lead to chronic stress and a possible misdiagnosis of PMDD.

Developing a plan to accept your ADHD symptoms and the idea of ADHD has an easy fix for finding confidence in your actions. And while that is easier than it sounds, the first step you can take is figuring out where you doubt yourself the most and where your lowest self-esteem points are.

Exercise Sixteen: Self-Reflection, Where Do You Doubt Yourself the Most?

We all have insecurities. They can nag us or tell us we are wrong, and when someone tells you something nice about yourself, insecurity can cause you not to believe them (more on that below). However, not everyone is insecure and allows those negative self-doubting words to bother them. If you find that you get anchored down into negative self-talk and let your brain walk all over your insecurity, this exercise is for you.

This is a self-reflection exercise where you will write down the negative thoughts and feelings about yourself, examine those, where they came from, why they are there, and work on shifting those into a new, more positive direction.

This exercise is not built to make you feel bad about yourself nor should you indulge the thoughts and emotions that come across when attempting this exercise. This is an objective study of why you feel what you feel when you feel it. If you find that the negative thoughts about yourself start to stick or make you feel low, you can swat them away like the bugs that they are. This exercise isn't meant to feed them, instead it's going to help you beat them.

Negative Thought One

_____

_____

_____

_____

Why do I think this way?

_____

_____

_____

_____

Where did it come from?

_____

_____

_____

_____

How can I rewrite the thought/feeling?

_____

_____

_____

_____

Negative Thought Two

_____

_____

_____

_____

Why do I think this way?

_____

_____

_____

_____

Where did it come from?

_____

_____

_____

_____

How can I rewrite the thought/feeling?

_____

_____

_____

_____

Negative Thought Three

_____

_____

_____

_____

Why do I think this way?

_____

_____

_____

_____

Where did it come from?

_____

_____

_____

_____

How can I rewrite the thought/feeling?

_____

_____

_____

_____

Negative Thought Four

_____

_____

_____

Why do I think this way?

_____

_____

_____

_____

Where did it come from?

_____

_____

_____

_____

How can I rewrite the thought/feeling?

_____

_____

_____

_____

Negative Thought Five

_____

_____

_____

_____

Why do I think this way?

_____

_____

_____

_____

Where did it come from?

_____

_____

_____

_____

_____

How can I rewrite the thought/feeling?

_____

_____

_____

_____

If you feel as though your emotions become unstable, it is always okay to stop the exercise above and take it slow. You will not have to do the memories all at once, nor will you have to do them alone. This exercise is something you can do with a therapist or counselor present.

Exercise Seventeen: Nice things People Say to Me—Here is Why I reject them.

There are a lot of things you might not be able to accept when someone says something nice. Whether it is about your appearance, kindness, work, or whatever, your first instinct may be to reject what someone says by waving it off, blushing, or saying, "No, I'm not." That's how many of us react, but that doesn't mean we should. Compliments and things others say about you are meant to make you feel good, so why don't you let yourself? What are you afraid will happen if you say, "Thank you, I appreciate the kind words." Nothing bad can come from it, and you are probably due to having someone say something nice because they mean it and because it is true.

There is an ongoing debate about how many good things we need to hear about erasing the bad things we tell ourselves. Some say the ratio is five nice things to every negative thing; others say three, and some say seven. Regardless of the number, the point is still the same: we do not treat ourselves very well.

But you will have to take that step to boost self-esteem and crush self-doubt. While this isn't always easy, it is good to learn to accept, take, and give genuine compliments. Although you must figure out why you reject them, you must first realize how you react to compliments.

This exercise is built to help you recognize your reaction to compliments. Like the previous exercises, you can recall memories of someone saying something nice. But then, remember what you said back. Was your first reaction a quick "No?" Did you wave your hand off and say, "You do not have to say that?" Or did you become embarrassed?

Each reaction is normal, especially when you don't want to hear something nice about yourself. You deserve to hear something nice about how you are. You are smart, strong, kind, funny, and so much more. However, if you have self-esteem issues, it will be much harder to take the compliment and sit with it than block the kindness coming your way.

Nice thing someone said to me:

_____
_____
_____
_____
_____
_____

My Reaction—what I said:

_____
_____
_____
_____
_____

How I felt:

_____
_____
_____
_____
_____

Nice thing someone said to me:

_____

_____

_____

_____

My Reaction—what I said:

_____

_____

_____

_____

How I felt:

_____

_____

_____

_____

_____

Nice thing someone said to me:

_____

_____

_____

My Reaction—what I said:

_____

_____

_____

How I felt:

_____

_____

_____

_____

Nice thing someone said to me:

_____

_____

_____

_____

My Reaction—what I said:

_____

_____

_____

_____

How I felt:

_____

_____

_____

Nice thing someone said to me:

_____

_____

_____

_____

My Reaction—what I said:

_____

_____

_____

_____

How I felt:

_____

_____

_____

_____

Nice thing someone said to me:

_____

_____

_____

_____

_____

My Reaction—what I said:

_____

_____

_____

_____

How I felt:

_____

_____

_____

_____

Nice thing someone said to me:

_____

_____

_____

_____

My Reaction—what I said:

_____

_____

_____

_____

How I felt:

_____

_____

_____

_____

Nice thing someone said to me:

_____

_____

_____

_____

My Reaction—what I said:

_____

_____

_____

_____

How I felt:

_____

_____

_____

_____

Nice thing someone said to me:

_____

_____

_____

_____

My Reaction—what I said:

_____

_____

_____

_____

How I felt:

_____

_____

_____

_____

Boost Your Self-Esteem and Crush Self-Doubt

Once you begin to see and feel your knee-jerk reactions to compliments, you may be able to understand why it is hard for you to accept that you are a nice person, but that only gets you over the threshold of confidence building. You will have to boost your confidence. Below is a list of activities to help you build your self-esteem. It is surprisingly much easier than it may seem. It takes a little self-care, a dash of intuition, and some building blocks. You will realize that helping yourself helps others, too (so you are really helping yourself to be selfless).

Dr. Peter Jaska, a journalist and clinical psychologist, discusses this in his article, "How to Regain Your Confidence: Life-Changing Strategies for Adults with ADHD." Jaska says:

When ADHD is managed well, this erosion of self-esteem can be prevented. Any emotional damage can also be repaired and reversed.

Remember: None of us are prisoners of our past, and it is never too late to change.

A strong program of treatment and ADHD management gives a person a fighting chance to manage their ADHD biology and behaviors reasonably (not perfectly) well. This is critical to ending a cycle of frustration and sense of failure (2022).

The past can weigh so heavily on us that we barely realize we are holding it in. These negative emotions can also affect how we look at the world and treat others. The cycle of frustration and sense of failure Jaska describes may be all too relevant to your life, but you have the power to pick yourself up and dust yourself off.

No one else is responsible for your emotions, self-confidence, or determination to accept you. People can support you, but you have to let them. You have to ask for help and hear what they are saying. When you are riddled with self-doubt and low self-esteem, it might not be easy to hear constructive things about you from others. However, it is important that you listen to them while you are building yourself up. You can still learn something even if you do not agree with what your support system is saying.

The statement above is not an excuse for someone to say negative and abusive things to you. Instead, it is an opportunity to take pieces of yourself and heal them.

Jaska also suggests what an effective treatment program can look like. This includes ADHD medication, behavioral therapy, ADHD coaching, and self-care like regular sleep, healthy nutrition, and physical activity (2022).

The article "How to Regain Your Confidence" discusses stopping negative thinking and provides the reader with eleven other tools to help yourself feel better and build your self-esteem in a healthy and strong place.

On negative thinking, Jaska says:

"One of the harmful aspects of low self-esteem is the loss of self-confidence and belief that you can change and grow. This feeling can be overcome, but it takes work and persistence. To get "unstuck," adults with ADHD have to recognize, challenge, and dismiss the negative thinking that comes with and contributes to low self-esteem.

Even when these negative messages feel natural, they must not be accepted as normal or healthy. View these messages as cognitive distortions instead. The battle for stronger self-esteem will be long, but it is a battle that can be won" (2022).

The negative messages we tell ourselves are interpretations of things we have learned from our past. Although they feel natural, they are not. Nor are these thoughts healthy. You can win the battle over your self-esteem, not that you will never have a negative idea of yourself again, but with the right tools, you will be able to deal with them more healthily and productively.

Below are eleven helpful tips to start building your confidence:

1.   As you accept and understand the biology of your ADHD, you can focus on changing your behavior. Do not think of the disorder as a negative label—you are not broken—that idea is a destructive stigma that diminishes your self-work and self-esteem.

2.   Your ADHD is not a defect of your character or a disease to be cured. ADHD is a neurobiological set of manageable symptoms.

3.   You are never too old to learn how to make your ADHD better. "I have tried everything" is not a valid excuse, and it is never true. There is always something else to try.

4. Appreciate your accomplishments by identifying them. If you are not sure what to pick, ask three people who support you for their genuine opinions.

5. Understand your strengths and weaknesses. You can ask friends or loved ones as well. Knowing where you can improve and are strong will help you build a better plan. Appreciate the strengths you have. Work on areas where you are weak by setting healthy and realistic goals.

6. Monitor, challenge and dismiss your negative self-talk. It is an ongoing battle and will be waged for as long as it is. While it will get easier over time, you will need persistent practice and the ability to identify the negativity you say to yourself.

7. Do not compare yourself to others. Do not do it. It is never a good idea and can easily spiral into a negative cycle. Anyone with low self-esteem will almost always find a way to be inferior.

8. Focus on solutions. When you identify your problem, you ask yourself, "What can I do about it," let the problem go and move forward to find the resolution.

9. Forget about the shoulda,' coulda,' woulda,'s. Anything in the past is best left there. You are working toward your future. Move forward with day-by-day progress in mind.

10. Find people who accept and love you for who you are—ADHD and all. Positive relationships will help you find a healthier frame of mind. Steer clear of isolating yourself from social and emotional places. Especially when you are feeling low.

11. Exercise, eat healthily, and sleep well. Taking care of your body will impact your mood incredibly (Jaksa, 2020).

Exercise Eighteen: Build a Positivity Plan

Below, write down one thing from each of the eleven tips that you can do to help yourself. Think about the SMART plan, and make your goals realistic, healthy, and time-relevant.

Plan for Tip One:

_____

_____

_____

Plan for Tip Two:

_____

_____

_____

Plan for Tip Three:

_____

_____

_____

Plan for Tip Four:

_____

_____

_____

Plan for Tip Five:

_____

_____

_____

Plan for Tip Six:

_____

_____

_____

Plan for Tip Seven:

_____

_____

_____

_____

Plan for Tip Eight:

_____

_____

_____

_____

Plan for Tip Nine:

_____

_____

_____

_____

Plan for Tip Ten:

_____

_____

_____

_____

Plan for Tip Eleven:

_____

_____

_____

_____

Once you start to build your confidence, other things in your life will begin to come together as well.

Managing ADHD and your hormones

Hormones play a huge role in every woman's life. When things get out of whack, they can mess up more than your mood. They can mess up how you sleep, how your body feels, how you think, what you crave to eat, and more. If you are a woman with ADHD, hormonal fluctuations can really touch every part of your world.

Dr. Ellen Lippman, a journalist and licensed clinical psychologist, studied girls and women with ADHD. She discovered that "the brain is a target organ for estrogen, where it impacts cognition, mood, and sleep (2012)."

The role hormones play in ADHD shifts drastically each month. Hormone levels fluctuate with the onset of menstruation. These changes include decreases and increases in estrogen, progesterone, and testosterone (CHADD, 2022).

These hormones also play a vital role in sexuality, emotions, reproduction, well-being, and health of the woman. Since test subjects have mostly been male in the past, hormone changes' effect on women with ADHD has not been studied as fluently as it can be, which is a topic that has been noted. Now, according to CHADD.org:

"A growing number of studies show that sex hormones play a role in regulating communications between brain cells and can negatively affect executive function (Barth et al., 2015). Rather than avoiding monthly fluctuations of hormones, Dr. Haimov-Kochman and Dr. Berger suggest new studies should focus on the subtle fluctuations and combinations of hormones that influence emotions and executive function to understand the role of hormones in ADHD.

The endocrine system comprises multiple glands that produce different kinds of hormones (Young, 2022). It is an interconnected system that is slow acting, with long-lasting impacts" (CHADD, 2022).

Now that a growing study shows the connection between sex hormones, brain cells, and their communication, scientists and researchers have begun to uncover how nuanced the ADHD mind is and how differently the disorder affects women.

What You Can Do About Hormones and ADHD

The thing about hormone levels is that you cannot see them. You do not know what they are, and it is rare to understand just how to manage them. When you couple hormones with ADHD, it can lead to a host of issues.

Several factors can affect hormone regulation. Psychosocial, environmental, and physiological factors, along with monthly hormone changes, not including menopause, perimenopause, and puberty, will impact how your symptoms present themselves (CHADD, 2022).

While studies of estrogen and other chemicals are less than ten years old, there are a few things you can do. As of now, you can get your hormone levels tested with your gynecologist or an endocrinologist. It is also a good idea to track your menstrual cycle and see how your cycle corresponds with your ADHD symptoms (CHADD, 2022).

Dr. Patricia Quinn, director of the National Center for Girls and Women with ADHD, wrote in her book *Understanding Women with ADHD* that:

"The average age of diagnosis for women with ADHD, who weren't diagnosed as children, is 36 to 38 years old. Before that time, girls and women were often misdiagnosed as having a mood disorder or an anxiety disorder. Even if these are secondary conditions, treating them does not get to the root of the problem, which is ADHD."

As such, doctors who do not see the connection between hormone levels and ADHD will not develop a proper treatment plan with you on how you can work within the boundaries of these things, which Quinn is looking to rectify.

In the article, "Women, Hormones, and ADHD," Laura Flynn McCarthy, a freelance writer specializing in children and women's health, writes about four stages of the hormonal life of women and offers ways to manage these symptoms.

As odd as it is to separate women into four parts of their life, understand that these are the times when hormone levels waver. While a woman is more than just pubescent, reproductive, pregnant, and menopausal, for the purposes of this section, that is how it is broken down.

Puberty

Girls start puberty between the ages of nine and eleven and, on average, get their period between eleven and fourteen. This is when hormones are bouncing through your body like a ping-pong ball and may have even been pegged as "raging" hormones when you were a child.

If you were a child diagnosed with ADHD and your parents put you on medication, the extra levels of progesterone and estrogen may have diminished how effective the medication was on ADHD. This erasure of help on medication may have even taken away your belief in medication.

Quinn says, "Studies have shown that estrogen may enhance a woman's response to amphetamine medications, but this effect may be diminished in the presence of progesterone (2002)."

Armed with this information, what do you do?

There are a few solutions.

Talk with your doctor or mental health specialist about different medications, their doses, and how long it takes to get used to each medication. Then you can pick the one that is best for you to try. Develop behavioral strategies, time management skills, and improve organization.

If you notice that your symptoms worsen over time or at certain times of the month, finish projects before these times hit, and maybe even discuss different self-care rituals to put in play the week before hormone levels flux (McCarthy & Novotni, "Women, Hormones, and ADHD," 2022).

Reproductive Years

If you are a woman in her reproductive years, you probably feel your ADHD symptoms a little more. Alternatively, if you just got diagnosed, you may now just be recognizing the inattentive, hyper, restless feeling you have close to or on your period has to do

with your ADHD and nothing to do with you as a person.

The average menstrual cycle is about twenty-eight days long. This count includes the first day of your period. During the first two weeks of your cycle, things go smoothly for women because this is when progesterone levels rise. The second two weeks are called the luteal phase. This is the third and fourth week when progesterone begins to fall past the beneficial levels, and estrogen's effects on your brain are reduced. This includes using estrogen stimulant medications (McCarthy & Novotni, "Women, Hormones, and ADHD," 2022).

Quinn believes that PMS is more acute in women who have ADHD. "Feelings of sadness and anxiety typically worsen in women with ADHD during this time (2002)."

Solutions for a woman in her reproductive years are as follows:

- Keep a log of your ADHD symptoms for three months—chart when you have symptoms and when they worsen during your cycle. See if you can find a pattern. Recent studies have found a variation from woman to woman. Symptoms can be as different as having heightened symptoms only one or two days of the month, whereas others have symptoms that get worse for ten days or more during the luteal phase.

- Medication can also help. Using a low-dose anti-anxiety or depressant up to two days before your period can help manage the highs and lows of emotions. Other women have found that increasing the dose of medication a few days before their symptoms heighten can help a balanced kick in. There are many ways that medication can help. Talk with your doctor or mental health professional to discuss your options. Do not change your dose without speaking to a doctor or mental health professional.

Pregnancy

During childbirth, hormone levels are incredibly out of whack. With pregnancy, your placenta will produce extra hormones to nourish itself and stimulate other glands, such as your thyroid and adrenal, which produce even more hormones (McCarthy & Novotni, "Women, Hormones, and ADHD," 2022). As your levels expand, you may begin to feel exhausted, have mood swings, and experience anxiety. However, when your estrogen levels kick in and increase again (usually after the first trimester), you should start feeling better—even if you have ADHD.

However, it may take a few days or a week to get your mood leveled out with each new trimester. And, after your child is born, hormone levels drop again. This drop can lead to postpartum depression and mood swings with any new mom, but women with ADHD are more prone to depression.

You and your doctor can evaluate your mood fluctuations in the months leading up to your due date. Keep track of everything you can, including how you react during each trimester shift, after you have the baby and how things are going when you are breastfeeding. There may be some issues with taking ADHD stimulants while breastfeeding, so you may have to rely on other help. However, certain antidepressant medications are safe, even while pregnant. Talk with your doctor about this to determine what is the best course of action for you.

Hormonal changes are unique to ADHD symptoms. You and your ADHD team of medical professionals know what is best for you. Some women have found that while pregnant or breastfeeding, going off their medication helped them function better due to the many hormone shifts of pregnancy.

Interestingly, hormonal changes during pregnancy can improve your ADHD symptoms. However, the hormonal benefits may be counterbalanced by the stress of a new infant, caring for other young children, pregnancy, and work. So it is an unusual kind of balancing act.

Perimenopause and Menopause

If you are a woman who has just landed in menopause or is perimenopausal, you will also have had hormonal shifts.

The average age of menopause is fifty-one, but many other things can trigger this change in women. If you have a full hysterectomy or have genetics that inspire perimenopausal symptoms, these can transition your hormones into chaos when you have ADHD.

This fluctuation happens because your estrogen levels will drop by roughly sixty-five percent between the onslaught of menopause. This decline can last up to ten years and is also part of perimenopause. The loss of your estrogen will lead to a reduction of dopamine and serotonin levels in your brain.

When you lose a steady and healthy stream of these hormones, you can become moody, sad, exhausted, and irritable. Your thoughts can also become fuzzy and lapse in your memory (McCarthy & Novotni, "Women, Hormones, and ADHD," 2022).

Quinn discusses this as the type of cognitive energy. She states, "Given a brain that, in effect, has less cognitive energy, to begin with, it can be especially hard for women with ADHD at this time in their life to concentrate and to make good decisions (2002)."

Solutions are similar to reproductive and puberty stages of life. However, they also include oral contraceptives, improving brain function, and balancing hormone levels. Once your period stops, you may be put on hormone-replacement therapy or can talk to your doctor about how this process can help you. Hormone-replacement therapy can happen for a few years. When you are on this type of therapy, Quinn explains that women on this type of therapy have been found to perform better on "cognitive testing, as well as on memory and reasoning-skills tests (2002)."

Many women do well with an estrogen-only treatment for up to four months and then follow it with ten days of progesterone.

It is important to seek the best course of treatment throughout each stage of your life. While ADHD symptoms can be managed, shifts in your hormones exacerbate symptoms and seem to come out of nowhere. Knowing what your body is going through by educating yourself about ADHD compared to symptoms and mood swings can help you keep up with anything that may throw a wrench in your normal behavior.

You can keep lists of your medications, chart your symptoms, be in touch with what is going on with your body, and continue to include medical and mental health professionals in your treatment. These actions will help you stay on track and prevent you from being blindsided (McCarthy & Novotni, Women, Hormones, and ADHD, 2022).

Exercise Eighteen: Are Your Hormones Out of Whack?

There are a few ways to track your hormones besides charting and journaling yourself. You can use a saliva test, give a blood sample to an endocrinologist, do a urine test, and take a blood spot test. Several of these tests are kits you can purchase and take at home. However, you may still need a doctor's help to review them.

If you are interested in keeping track of your hormones with a journal, you can build a period tracker by taking the next three to six months and writing about it. Keep your layout simple, so it is easy for you to read and remember.

You can create a physical chart in a notebook with month and date columns. Questions to answer in your journal are as follows:

- List period symptoms. Think about your symptoms, including cravings, pain, mood shifts, etc.

- Track your mood during each cycle. You can do this with simple icons, emoji stickers, or something similar.

- Create a list of self-care tips you can use when feeling low. Having a list of ideas about hygiene, healthy food, meditation, relaxation, and more will help you when you might forget (Dua, 2022).

- Find out when ovulation is and record those dates. You can find this out with a home kit or with the help of a doctor.

- If you have sex, make sure to record the dates. This is a good practice to have even if you are not trying to get pregnant.

If you prefer technology because of notifications and reminders, there are many types of apps for your phone that you can download and use.

Exercise Nineteen: Finding Natural Ways to Help with Hormones

While you can keep track of your hormone swings, you can also find healthy, non-medical ways to keep your hormone levels on track. These methods can include getting proper sleep, good self-care rituals, mindfulness, exercise, and food. Below is a list of helpful tips to find better cooking methods and some ideas to help keep yourself balanced when your hormones and symptoms intermix.

Tips to Follow

Eating clean, whole foods is not the only way to keep your hormone levels in check. Read below for some other tips to help yourself out.

- **Get your protein**—food is essential to helping your body work well. To ensure it works at its highest capacity, ensure you are eating enough protein at each meal. Protein provides crucial amino acids that your body is unable to make. Protein also helps produce hormones called peptides. Endocrine glands make peptides with the help of amino acids. With enough peptides, you will have a good metabolism, appetite, stress management, growth, and reproduction. Try for a minimum of twenty to thirty grams of protein a day.

- **Exercise is important**—not only does exercise burn excess ADHD energy and produce chemicals to help you think more clearly, but it also encourages strong hormonal health. Physical activity improves blood flow to your muscles and increases sensitivity in hormone receptors, which helps reduce insulin levels and fights against possible insulin resistance.

- **Give yourself good gut health**—the gut microbiome (the ecology of your gut) modulates insulin resistance and how full you feel. This area also regulates hormones with over 100 trillion good bacteria. These bacteria can produce many metabolites, which can affect hormone health in a positive or negative way. Pump your body up with pro- and prebiotics to ensure you have healthy bacteria in your gut.

- **Lower your sugars**—not all sugars are bad, but minimizing your sugar intake, especially refined sugar, corn syrup, agave, etc., can severely increase your energy levels and regulate your hormones to a healthy place. Long-term use of any of the items above can promote insulin resistance and make it harder for you to lose weight, eat right, and take care of your hormonal health.

- **Stress Reduction**—lowering your stress levels will revive your hormones in wonderful ways. When your body goes through increased amounts of long-term stress, your cortisol levels will spike and continue to produce until the stress dissipates. However, chronic stress can confuse your system and impair feedback, making your body unsure of what hormones it needs to work properly.

- **Sleep tight**—if you are not getting enough restorative sleep, no amount of healthy food or working out will help your hormones. In fact, poor sleep is linked to imbalances in many hormones like cortisol, ghrelin, HGH, and leptin (Cooper et al., 2018; Lang, 2022).

Conclusion

Depending on the hormone levels within your body, tips, tricks, and food changes can help you level the playing field between medicine, ADHD, and hormones. These items can help you reduce stress, boost your energy, and help you think more clearly.

Taking notes and tracking your menstrual cycles with mood and ADHD symptoms can also help you figure out when you need the most work in what areas.

Reviewing this section will help keep you on top of any emotional regulations, rejection sensitivity, and hormonal issues that may arise in the future. The more you can build self-awareness, the easier time you will have to find a solution to the issue.

The next chapter will discuss more about cleaning, organizing, and decluttering your ADHD lifestyle.

CHAPTER FIVE

Cleaning, Organizing, & Decluttering

What does your home look like?

Do you live in an environment where papers are strewn about, dirty dishes are piled in your sink, and food sits in your refrigerator rotting and forgotten about? If this sounds familiar, you are not alone.

We all struggle to keep our places and spaces clean, especially when busy. If kids are involved, keeping a clean house after they start crawling is nearly impossible. If there is an issue of chronic messiness and disorganization, ADHD makes cleaning and organizing even harder (Davis & Hill, 2022).

Besides hyperactivity, ADHD is synonymous with disorganization and planning. Although, honestly, it is not because of anything you have done. Planning, organizing, and cleaning are all part of executive function, and as discussed in Chapter Three, executive dysfunction is caused by a disconnect between the communication synapses in your brain. When these circuits miscommunicate, they will affect the main skills driven by the executive function.

The three main deficits with executive dysfunction involve self-motivation, planning and problem solving, and non-verbal working memory (Barkley & Novotni, 2022). If you have issues with any of these things, remembering to motivate yourself to clean and plan for decluttering your home can be an issue for anyone with ADHD.

Many women have reported not having people over to their homes because they are embarrassed about how it looks. They worry they do not fit the "good" housekeeper role, like so many other women do—another downfall of a patriarchal society. Instead of focusing on cleaning, you may throw your energy into buying things (especially if you have impulsive-hyperactive ADHD) to put around the house to look nice, which only encourages more clutter.

You may have days where you can throw yourself into cleaning, but it can quickly get overwhelming when you realize just how much you have to clean. Plus, if you get distracted by a few things here and there, you may forget entirely that your focus is to clean the house.

If you feel you are ready to flip your neurodivergent brain on its side and conquer the stereotypical ADHD idea that no one with the disorder can live an organized life, read through the section below.

However, before you start, follow the next few tips to eliminate the pressure to be "clean."

1. Take each project one at a time.

2. Break this project into chunks.

3. Use a timer—set it for ten or fifteen minutes to start. Clean for that amount of time and go do something else.

4. Try this practice every day.

5. Build a SMART goal list and create some SMART goals.

    a. Specific

    b. Measurable

    c. Achievable

    d. Realistic

    e. Timely

The worst thing you can do to yourself is put pressure on the idea of decluttering, cleaning, and organizing. Eliminate words like "should" and "have to" from your cleaning vocabulary. Do not say that your house will "never" be dirty again. Strike these absolute terms to avoid adding that extra stress to a situation. Unrealistic expectations will only set you up for failure, knocking you down. You deserve to keep up and get the life you want. If cleaning, organizing, and decluttering your house is part of that goal, then it is time to start.

The Problem With Clutter & How to Organize

Many problems come with clutter and disorganization. While some issues are innocuous (but frustrating), like losing your keys, glasses, television remote, etc., others can be pretty big, like forgetting appointments, misplacing important documents, and losing bills that need to be paid.

One of the most important steps, if not the most crucial, is to separate yourself from the mess. You are not lazy, dirty, or unclean. Realize that it is not your fault, it is merely the way your brain developed, and you can do things to correct it. Many women with ADHD have this symptom, and it has been noted that many women feel lonely or like an oddity when they just haven't found the best way to work with their brains.

Our book, "Women with ADHD," discusses the emotional calculations that cleaning takes. We say:

"Cleaning with ADHD requires an emotional and logical preparation to begin the task. Once you start, you must follow through with the ideas and complete them. This mental stimulation is exactly the opposite of what an ADHD brain does.

Just because this type of planning works against the ADHD mind does not mean that you will never live in a home that is clean and free of any clutter. However unrealistic it may seem, you CAN work a cleaning routine into your daily life (Davis & Hill, 2022)."

That is great if you are already on a behavioral plan and moving forward. Suppose you have gotten on medication and can think and function with clearer intentions. That is amazing. Alternatively, if you are in the beginning stages of your ADHD education, that is wonderful too. You can always learn more no matter what stage you are in the ADHD process.

Exercise Twenty: Your Umbrella Goals

After you have separated yourself from the clutter and the disorganization, you can set a goal. What would you like it to be? Your cleaning goal can be to get rid of excess clutter in your home, you can have a desire to find important objects with ease, or you can just set your intentions to improve the space you live in.

Think of this goal as the open part of an umbrella. Everything you want to put under the "big" goal will have to do with your main goal. For instance, if you want to improve your living space, you will add other tiers under the umbrella goal and will continue to chunk everything together until they are manageable pieces for your life.

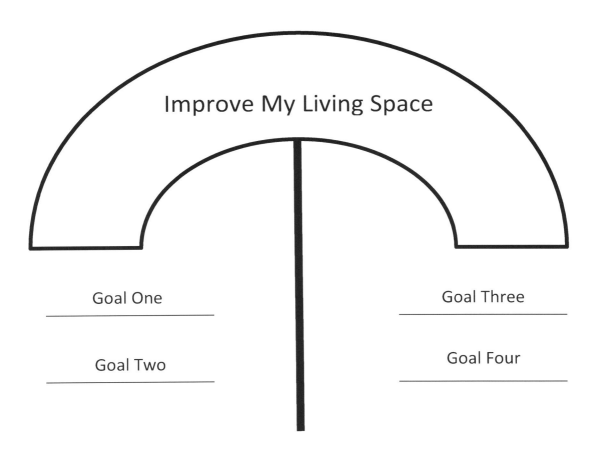

Each goal you have under your main goal will be broken down. If you have four goals of "improving my living space," think about what it will look like.

Example Umbrella Goal

- Goal One—Keep the kitchen clean.

    ○ Rinse the dishes right after use and put them in the dishwasher (15 minutes).

    ○ Run the dishwasher at least once a day.

    ○ Clean the dishwasher out each day (10 minutes).

    ○ Wipe down counters every day (5 minutes).

    ○ Sweep the floor with a broom every other day (15 minutes).

        ■ Choose two days.

        ● Goal Two—Keep the bedroom clean.

    ○ Make bed every day (3 minutes).

    ○ Dust dressers, etc., once a week (15 minutes).

    ○ Vacuum once a week (30 minutes).

    ○ Put all clothes away (15 minutes).

    ○ Do laundry once a week.

        ■ Choose a day.

    ○ Take out any non-relevant items from the bedroom.

        ■ List items not relevant for sleeping, resting or getting ready for the day.

- Goal Three—pets.

    ○ Clean cat litter daily (7 minutes).

- Pick the time before/after work.

- Have kids do it after school.

○ Pick up dog poop daily (7 minutes).

- Pick time.

○ Take a dog for a walk every day (45 minutes).

- Pick time.

○ Clean out birdcage every week (15 minutes).

- Pick a day to do this.

○ Feed pets every day at a certain time (5 minutes).

- Pick time.

○ Give them water every day at a certain time (5 minutes).

- Pick time.

● Goal Four—get rid of clutter.

○ Start in the living room.

- Clean one corner of the room a day for fifteen minutes.

- Put things in boxes to donate.

○ Take boxes to the donation bin and pick a deadline.

- If I have not used or seen it in six months, it is time to donate it or throw it away.

- Get a bin for extra blankets, pillows, etc.

○ Set a deadline to wash, fold, and store these.

- Dust shelves (15 minutes).

- Sweep floors (15 minutes).

- Organize pictures, videos, music, etc., (45 minutes).

○ Go to the bathroom.

- Clean one area daily for fifteen minutes until the entire bathroom is clutter-free.

○ Clear away old medications, nail polish, makeup, hair supplies, cleaning products, etc.

○ Put items in bags to be thrown out.

○ Dispose of old cleaning products appropriately.

- Clean toilet (10 minutes).

- Clean bathtub/shower (15 minutes).

- Clean off counter space and leave only toothbrushes and hand soap on the counter. Everything else gets put away in the cabinet or closet.

- Wash or sweep the rug/floor (20-30 minutes).

- Put a fresh hand towel out once a week unless you need to do it sooner.

○ Pick a day.

○ Add a dirty hand towel to the laundry.

Now It is Your Turn: Place your goal at the top of the list. Fill in the rest of the information in the goals below. Once you complete this list, figure out what goal you want to begin with first, and make sure to write down how long each task is expected to take. That way, you can set a timer for the tasks in the beginning and get yourself into the best practice possible.

Main goal: _____

- Goal One: _____

  - Task_____(time____)

    - subtask_____(time____)

    - subtask_____(time____)

    - subtask_____(time____)

  - Task_____(time____)

    - subtask_____(time____)

    - subtask_____(time____)

    - subtask_____(time____)

  - Task_____(time____)

    - subtask_____(time____)

    - subtask_____(time____)

    - subtask_____(time____)

  - Task_____(time____)

    - subtask_____(time____)

    - subtask_____(time____)

    - subtask_____(time____)

- Goal Two: _____

  - Task_____(time____)

    - subtask_____(time____)

- ■ subtask_____(time____)

- ■ subtask_____(time____)

- ○ Task_____(time____)

  - ■ subtask_____(time____)

  - ■ subtask_____(time____)

  - ■ subtask_____(time____)

- ○ Task_____(time____)

  - ■ subtask_____(time____)

  - ■ subtask_____(time____)

  - ■ subtask_____(time____)

- ○ Task_____(time____)

  - ■ subtask_____(time____)

  - ■ subtask_____(time____)

  - ■ subtask_____(time____)

- • Goal Three: _____

  - ○ Task_____(time____)

    - ■ subtask_____(time____)

    - ■ subtask_____(time____)

    - ■ subtask_____(time____)

  - ○ Task_____(time____)

    - ■ subtask_____(time____)

- ■ subtask_____ (time_____)

- ■ subtask_____ (time_____)

- ○ Task_____ (time_____)

  - ■ subtask_____ (time_____)

  - ■ subtask_____ (time_____)

  - ■ subtask_____ (time_____)

- ○ Task_____ (time_____)

  - ■ subtask_____ (time_____)

  - ■ subtask_____ (time_____)

  - ■ subtask_____ (time_____)

- ● Goal Four:

  - ○ Task_____ (time_____)

    - ■ subtask_____ (time_____)

    - ■ subtask_____ (time_____)

    - ■ subtask_____ (time_____)

  - ○ Task_____ (time_____)

    - ■ subtask_____ (time_____)

    - ■ subtask_____ (time_____)

    - ■ subtask_____ (time_____)

  - ○ Task_____ (time_____)

    - ■ subtask_____ (time_____)

- subtask_____(time____)

- subtask_____(time____)

  ○ Task_____(time____)

    - subtask_____(time____)

    - subtask_____(time____)

    - subtask_____(time____)

A Home that fits your ADHD

Look around your home. Do you see clutter?

You might not recognize that the big piles of paper stashed in the corner of your living room or the kitchen counter filled with utensils, tchotchkes, and boxed foods are clutter. You might think, "If I can see the floor, my home is clean (Davis & Hill, 2022)."

That is normal for ADHD.

The problem happens when your peripheral vision decides that the clutter is too overwhelming to look at, and you go "clutter-blind." Just because you can see the floor in your home does not mean that your cleaning habits are up to snuff or that your house is clean.

To start a clutter-free life, you will have to look at most of the things in your house. It turns out that you can get rid of most of them.

Thinking of throwing away anything may give you heart palpitations. Nothing bad will happen, even if it seems like a bad idea. You are going to try to do things. It will feel awkward and a bit uncomfortable, like wearing a dress that makes you look weird, or putting on a new, brighter lipstick shade when you are used to going neutral. It does not mean that you will always feel uncomfortable. It means that you need to get used to them. It is time to stand out. Wear that dress. Put on that lipstick. Create a clutter-free space for yourself.

A clean, clutter-free environment means a cleaner and less cluttered mind. Knowing what to throw out and what to keep may sound overwhelming, but ask yourself this: Would taking care of a specific item in the way it was meant to be taken care of be worth your time and effort?

If you answer this question with "yes," keep it. If you answer "no," you know what to do: donate it or throw it away. There are many people who may not have what you do and may need it. Always consider donating if the object is in good condition and you know it can get love and use somewhere else.

You will probably answer "no" more often than "yes." This honesty will help you cut down on having too much clutter faster than you realize. The less you have, the less time there will be to keep it organized and clean (Cantrell, 2022).

Exercise Twenty-One: What and Where is Your Clutter?

You must take off the clutter blinds and look at each room. What do you see? Can you make a list of items that look like they could be cluttered, even if you are sure?

- Dead plants

- Dirty or broken trinkets & tchotchkes

- Piles of paper

- Cardboard boxes from online orders

- Food wrappers

- Books

- Cans

- Bottles

- Crafting supplies that you are always meaning to use

- Holiday decorations to be put away

- Picture frames that need hung up

- Trophies, Awards, Certificates

- Pet supplies

- Cooking supplies

- Body, hygiene, & makeup products

- Receipts

- Fast food leftovers

- Dirty paper towels
- Cleaning supplies
- Old sponges
- Shoes
- Computer supplies
- And more

You can fill out the spaces below if you need to list the clutter in each room. The above examples can provide a good foundation to know what to look for, but it can be anything from dryer lint and sheets to clothes and accessories strewn about the floor.

- Living Room: _____

  ○ Corner One

  ■ _____

  ■ _____

  ■ _____

  ■ _____

  ■ _____

  ○ Corner Two

  ■ _____

  ■ _____

  ■ _____

  ■ _____

  ■ _____

○   Corner Three

   ■   _____

   ■   _____

   ■   _____

   ■   _____

   ■   _____

○   Corner Four

   ■   _____

   ■   _____

   ■   _____

   ■   _____

   ■   _____

●   Bathroom: _____

○   Corner One

   ■   _____

   ■   _____

   ■   _____

   ■   _____

   ■   _____

○   Corner Two

    ■   _____

    ■   _____

    ■   _____

    ■   _____

    ■   _____

○   Corner Three

    ■   _____

    ■   _____

    ■   _____

    ■   _____

    ■   _____

○   Corner Four

    ■   _____

    ■   _____

    ■   _____

    ■   _____

    ■   _____

●   Bedroom One: _____

○   Corner One

     ■   _____

     ■   _____

     ■   _____

     ■   _____

     ■   _____

○   Corner Two

     ■   _____

     ■   _____

     ■   _____

     ■   _____

     ■   _____

○   Corner Three

     ■   _____

     ■   _____

     ■   _____

     ■   _____

     ■   _____

○   Corner Four

     ■   _____

- ■ _____
- ■ _____
- ■ _____
- ■ _____

- ●   Bedroom Two: _____

  ○   Corner One

- ■ _____
- ■ _____
- ■ _____
- ■ _____
- ■ _____

  ○   Corner Two

- ■ _____
- ■ _____
- ■ _____
- ■ _____
- ■ _____

  ○   Corner Three

- ■ _____
- ■ _____

- ■ _____
- ■ _____
- ■ _____

- ○ Corner Four

- ■ _____
- ■ _____
- ■ _____
- ■ _____
- ■ _____

- ● Bedroom Three: _____

- ○ Corner One

- ■ _____
- ■ _____
- ■ _____
- ■ _____
- ■ _____

- ○ Corner Two

- ■ _____
- ■ _____
- ■ _____

- ■ _____

- ■ _____

- ■ _____

○   Corner Three

- ■ _____

- ■ _____

- ■ _____

- ■ _____

- ■ _____

○   Corner Four

- ■ _____

- ■ _____

- ■ _____

- ■ _____

- ■ _____

●   Kitchen: _____

○   Corner One

- ■ _____

- ■ _____

- ■ _____

- ■ _____
- ■ _____
- ■ _____

- ○ Corner Two

  - ■ _____
  - ■ _____
  - ■ _____
  - ■ _____
  - ■ _____

- ○ Corner Three

  - ■ _____
  - ■ _____
  - ■ _____
  - ■ _____
  - ■ _____

- ○ Corner Four

  - ■ _____
  - ■ _____
  - ■ _____
  - ■ _____

- ■ _____

- ●   Extra Room: _____

- ○   Corner One

  - ■ _____

  - ■ _____

  - ■ _____

  - ■ _____

  - ■ _____

- ○   Corner Two

  - ■ _____

  - ■ _____

  - ■ _____

  - ■ _____

  - ■ _____

- ○   Corner Three

  - ■ _____

  - ■ _____

  - ■ _____

  - ■ _____

  - ■ _____

○   Corner Four

- ■   _____

- ■   _____

- ■   _____

- ■   _____

- ■   _____

●   Extra Room: _____

○   Corner One

- ■   _____

- ■   _____

- ■   _____

- ■   _____

- ■   _____

○   Corner Two

- ■   _____

- ■   _____

- ■   _____

- ■   _____

- ■   _____

- ○   Corner Three

  - ■ _____

  - ■ _____

  - ■ _____

  - ■ _____

  - ■ _____

- ○   Corner Four

  - ■ _____

  - ■ _____

  - ■ _____

  - ■ _____

  - ■ _____

Exercise Twenty-Two: Purging Your Clutter

Once you have an idea of what your clutter is, you can start to purge the clutter.

Ask yourself a few things:

- **What are my target areas**? You can pinpoint these by finding spots in your home that gather the most mess. Remember you live in this space and know what works best for you (or do not be afraid to try new things). Find what feels the most comfortable and set that as your standard.

- **Where can I clean to make things easier on myself**—Where do you spend the most time? Are you in the kitchen, living room, office, etc.?

- **What is your biggest problem area**—Do you have too many shoes? Are you finding that you have piles of paper everywhere?

- **Where do you want to start**—Sometimes, cleaning the biggest area will be the most overwhelming. Pick where you are most comfortable starting and go for it. You can set a timer so you do not feel trapped by clutter and stick to it, so you do not get distracted or become hyperfocused and burn out.

Below is a list to help you start on your clutter-free journey. Check some ideas that seem like they would work best for you and try them out (Cantrell, 2022; Davis & Hill, 2022).

- **Clothes**—Do your clothes get tossed on the floor? Over a bench? Left in the bathroom?

- Add hooks to your doors to hang the clothes you plan on wearing again before washing.

For example, hanging things like pajamas on a hook can alleviate the stress of having clothes build up on the floor or save you from looking for them when you are getting ready for bed.

- Keep a laundry basket in these areas if you do not wear clothes a second time, but they are thrown over the floor in your bathroom, laundry room, or bedroom. Take (and keep) the lid off to make it even easier.

If you have issues with throwing clothes on the floor, even after they are clean, dedicate one or two baskets to clean clothes only. Keep clean clothes in these baskets until you are ready to fold them—but still, make folding your clothes a priority in your routine.

- **Kitchen**—What are your biggest problem areas in the kitchen? Are the counters cleaned off? Do you have coffee accessories thrown everywhere? Do fruit and spices get tossed into the same place?

- To solve this problem, get baskets. Lots of baskets. Do this after you clear the counters and tables off.

Keep your coffee supplies in one basket. Your fruit in another. Your spices in a third, and so on. Get a basket for every item you have put away. Give each basket of items a specific place on your counter or table.

For example, keep fruit near the snack drawers or other places you have food.

- Use labels to help you remember what is where and what to use.

- Add a list of items you need to buy each time you run out. They have some great ones that are also magnets for you to stick to your refrigerator.

- **Desk**—Do you have papers that pile up everywhere? Can you not find the proper tools needed to complete a task?

- Get yourself a few filing shelves with no lids. Keep two on your desk—one for "to-read" items and one for "read" items.

Put your pencils, paperclips, rubber bands, post-it notes, etc., in baskets.

- Get an open shelving unit to add everything to. Clean it off every week or twice a month.

Throw away things you do not need, file what you need, and keep a color-coded system for each shelf (blue means bills, green means cleaning supplies, etc.)

- Get a large calendar to add your deadlines. Set the calendar on your desk, so it is always in view (Cantrell, 2022; Davis & Hill, 2022).

- **Trash**—Where does most trash wind up?

- Put a garbage can close to that area. Do not hide it, do not keep a lid on it—keep it near where garbage piles up and make it easy for yourself to throw things away instead of leaving them on the floor, table, counter, etc.

For example, if you eat snacks in front of the TV, put a can next to the couch to throw the wrappers into the garbage can as soon as you eat the snack.

- Set an alarm each day, or twice a day if needed, then stand up from your area and pick up any trash that has accrued (Cantrell, 2022; Davis & Hill, 2022).

Tackle each corner of each room one day a week for a set amount of time until each area has been decluttered. If you use fifteen minutes a day, that is a short burst of time that you set for yourself and can be manageable. Unless you find decluttering your space a Zen experience, stay away from trying to do two-hour chunks or more. You are trying to create a healthy balance for yourself.

Clutter does not have to go away all at once. The important thing with this practice is building a clutter-free environment and learning to have healthy cleaning habits.

Exercise Twenty-Three: Chore Charts and Rewards Lists

The purpose of creating a chore chart and reward list is simple. You will see it. With ADHD, you may have an issue called "object permanence." This idea is similar to, but not exactly, the object permanence we learn as children when we play "peek-a-boo."

If something is out of sight with the ADHD brain, it may be out of mind. That does not mean you do not realize it is gone completely or forever, but it does mean that until you see it again, you will forget it is even there.

There are many ways to create chore charts and reward lists. One example of each is below. If you have a better idea that will suit your lifestyle and start you on the visualization journey, feel free to use it! See the example below, you can check off each day you do the chore and cross out, or X the days you did not have to.

Daily Chores

	M	Tu	W	Th	F	Sa	Su
Wash the dishes/dishwasher	😀	😠	☐	🤩	😫	☐	🤓

The example above shows that emoji are for more fun touch, but you can use anything that your heart fancies.

The other chart is for rewards, which are completely up to you. Make a list of items you want to do, buy, eat, play, etc. Then set appropriate rewards once you have finished

decluttering a room, or hit four out of seven days on your chore chart.

Make a list like the one below. Don't forget to add what you have to do to get the reward!

Reward List

	Reward	M	Tu	W	Th	F	Sa	Su
Did chores five days in a row	Movie Night	✦	✦	✦	✦	✦	✦	✦
I got all four corners of clutter cleaned in the living room	Buy a new item							
Got the first floor cleaned	Go to the spa							

Did chores for two weeks in a row	Go to dinner at your favorite restaurant. Order whatever you want.						

After you have used a reward, make sure to reset it. Also, keep a list handy of things you would like rewards for. Entertainment, dining, outdoor experiences, and bath time can all be used. Take the things you love to do the most and leverage them to help you clean, declutter, and make your space more ADHD breathable.

Conclusion

Learning how to declutter, clean, and organize your life is going to help your ADHD situate itself in a new and exciting way. You'll start to be able to see the benefits of having a clean space, being organized in each part of your life, and enjoying the rewards that come your way.

Chapter Six will give you a few ideas how to work with ADHD, have friends, build a career, and keep healthy financial practices.

CHAPTER SIX

ADHD & Relationships

Social life, career, and financial health are all vital elements for living a more focused-driven life. When something is out of whack, you can work on it easily, but if everything seems as though it piles up, falls over, swirls around, and creates chaos, these things may seem as though they are impossible to touch. They are not, but first, you need to know where to start.

Women with ADHD tend to be socially isolated more because they feel as though they have a weakened understanding of how to be social. You do not, but that is the consensus in research and evidence found in studies (Novotni, 2022).

Many women responded that they feel exposed and vulnerable in the areas below:

- No social connections with acquaintances, business associates, and friends.

- How to master multi-tasking by switching between family, home, work, and friends.

- An inability to ask for help or assert their news.

- Feeling sadness due to a lack of positive social interaction leads to isolation (Novotni, 2022).

You can avoid staying in an isolated frame of mind, but you will have to do a few things and help shake yourself out of those places where you are stuck.

Exercise Twenty-Four: Tips and Tricks for Stepping out of Social Isolation

- **Do not be too hard on yourself**. No one learns social skills in school. There are no "do's" and "don'ts" of how to behave in situations, but society tells each other that we should know what to do and when to do it. If you come across people like this, know that you can create healthy boundaries and do not need to develop a deeper friendship with them. We are all flawed, and anyone who says differently is lying to themselves.

- **Focus on people who will give you honest, kind, and unconditional feedback**. Although it may be hard to ask someone what social skills you need to improve on if you are genuine in your desire to change and approach them with an open mind, you can give yourself an amazing opportunity for growth and change (Davis & Hill, 2022).

- **Multi-task your relationships**. Luckily, ADHD allows you to be a stellar multi-tasker. Although it can be hard with the pressures life puts on you, make sure to spend some time with your friends. If you have to carve out time purposefully, you must do that. With everything you have going on, you will drain yourself easily if you do not make time for yourself and some people who do not rely on you (aka friends!) for everything.

- **Women do not need to "have it all," "do it all," and "be it all."** That is way too much pressure to put on yourself, and if people in your life are making you feel that way, then you can reassess those healthy boundaries. Delegation and self-care are the right way to have a healthy mental state. If you have children and a spouse, everyone living in the family can have tasks.

- **Learn how to assert yourself, even if you hate conflict**. You are always going to come across things that are uncomfortable or even those you downright hate. You may be in the practice of pushing things down or talking yourself into being the person to blame, but that is not the case. It shows healthy boundaries and confidence in yourself when you know how to say, "I do not like this." Try to find friends and partners whom you can learn to ask for what you want without judgment or friction. If you are afraid, you can always precursor that information by saying, "I am very uncomfortable, but I would like to talk to you."

- **Understand that ADHD is going to give you strong feelings**. Remember that you are not only a woman with ADHD but also a woman with feelings. People in your life may tell you that you react strongly about things. These actions are okay, but make sure to assess them with a mental health professional to see if they are associated with emotional dysregulation or just mere feelings you feel (Davis & Hill, 2022).

The Challenges of Friendship

Exercise Twenty-Five: What Type of Friend are You?

It's almost redundant to say that ADHD has a laundry list of items that infringe on your life, but it touches on your social life too. Maintaining healthy friendships where both people put the relationship may heighten some of your ADHD symptoms without you even realizing it. Think about what kind of friend you are, do you feel any of the items listed below? Check the boxes that sound like you and add in some extra ones in the space if they aren't listed.

- Feeling Overwhelmed

- Getting Bored

- Inconsistency With Friendships

- Poor Memory

- Your Self-Esteem

- Your Depression & Anxiety

- Lack of Friends Equals a Lack of Acceptance.

- The Shame of Friendship.

- Reciprocating is Difficult.

- Time Issues

- Your Phone is Your Lifeline.

- Your Thoughts May Not Cooperate (Broadbent, 2022).

- _____

- _____

- _____

-

Once you figure out what type of issues you may have with friendships, review the ADHD symptoms and see if any of the actions in the different ADHD kinds sound similar to how you have treated your friends:

Women with Hyperactive-Impulsive ADHD will:

- Get bored easily

- Interrupt others

- Ignore social rules

- Blurt out negative criticism

- Control the conversations

- Focus the conversation on themselves

- Enhance their stimulation level with substances

- End frustrating relationships.

Women with Inattentive ADHD will:

- Be overwhelmed by social and emotional demands.

- Avoid impromptu social gatherings.

- Have anxiety in unfamiliar environments (especially with many people).

- Second-guess and censor their feelings and responses if they feel conflict coming.

- Create flaws to have others avoid them, so they do not have to avoid others.

- Label mistakes as character flaws.

- Assume everyone will reject or criticize them (Davis & Hill, 2022).

-

Does any of this sound like you? Can you think of ways to work with them or challenge your ideas? Do you think you may be in denial of what kind of friend you are?

Think about it and write those thoughts in your journal or the space below.

_____

_____

_____

_____

_____

_____

Exercise Twenty-Six: Some Social Strategies to Consider

See the questions below. Answer them in the best way you know how to. If you are unsure, write your thoughts, then go over them with a trusted friend, partner, counselor, or mental health professional.

● How can you accept yourself fully? Finding a way to look at yourself with respect, value, and love will attract some amazing people. What are a few ways to help yourself?

_____

_____

_____

_____

_____

_____

_____

● How can technology help your friendships? With everything that technology offers, including notifications, alarms, and reminders, how could you use your smartphone to help you keep in touch with your people? For example, emails, texts, and calendars are a great start.

_____

_____

_____

_____

_____

_____

_____

● How comfortable are you talking about your ADHD? Remember, everyone has flaws, your ADHD does not have to be considered one of them, but the symptoms bring certain challenges to the friendship table. Name some of those items below. If you are not comfortable talking about your ADHD with a certain friend, think about if you are uncomfortable with your ADHD or maybe worried that your friend will not accept you for you. If the response is the latter, you might want to think about distancing yourself from that person.

_____

_____

_____

_____

_____

_____

_____

●   Do you know what your ADHD triggers are? Your actions, thoughts, and words may seem as though they come out of nowhere when there is a moment of a trigger that could boost your ADHD symptoms. Write some triggers below, what you can do when faced with them, and how you can rebound if you cannot.

_____

_____

_____

_____

_____

_____

_____

●   Do you know what activities you like to do most? If you make plans with your friends, think about doing something where you can move around. That would give you the optimal time to burn energy and build bonds with a friend or group of friends. Write some ideas of things you like to do that are active below.

_____

_____

_____

_____

_____

_____

_____

• If you want to reciprocate and host an event at your place, you should! But remember to take things slowly. Start small and work your way up to bigger and better events. Write some ideas below to see how incredible your dinner party, brunch, or game night can be. Remember that everyone is an adult and can bring something to the gathering, do not put everything all on yourself. That is the perfect way to burn out before you start.

_____

_____

_____

_____

_____

_____

_____

Friendly Advice: Cut some slack and give yourself time to transition into new habits. Remember to be flexible with your friends as well as your actions. Although you have ADHD, it should not stop you from remembering that other people's lives, interests, families, feelings, and more are just as important as yours.

When you build strong relationships with others, you will find a vital part of your life that you have missed.

Your Relationship with Romance

ADHD will affect how you look at a partner and how your partner looks at you. While it can be fun and exciting at first, once the shine wears off, you may wonder what to do next, especially if you want to stay in the relationship and develop it into something deeper.

Look at the challenge below. Does this sound like something you have done with a romantic partner? For a woman in a serious relationship, distractions can come from the simplest places. An example taken from CHADD.org goes something like this:

Partner without ADHD: "Hey, hon—do you want to watch a movie?"

Partner with ADHD: "Sure, I will go make popcorn."

- She walks to the kitchen to make popcorn but sees clothes and toys lying on the floor in the den. She picks them up and takes them to her child's room to put them away.

- She sees that her child forgot to put their toothbrush away and left it on their desk. Even though she is annoyed with her child's inability to put things away, she picks them up and takes them to the bathroom (the clothes and toys are forgotten about).

- She realizes it needs to be cleaned up when she gets to the bathroom. She pulls out the cleaning supplies and begins wiping down the counter.

- Her partner starts looking for her throughout the house and finds her cleaning the bathroom. The partner sees her doing other things, popcorn still not made, and believes she never wanted to watch the movie in the first place (CHADD, 2018; Davis & Hill, 2022).

While none of the items above were done intentionally to hurt your partner, the steady stream of distractions allowed the woman with ADHD to lose her way from the original goal of spending romantic time together. The book Women with ADHD states,

"If you are aware of your ADHD and have open communication with your partner about it, this instance might not be a big deal—it might even be expected. However, if your ADHD is undiagnosed, if this type of event happens often, or if you are not transparent with your partner, they may begin to see it as an issue and believe you don't want to spend time with them (Davis & Hill, 2022)."

Exercise Twenty-Seven: Map Out a Distraction Moment

Think about the example above. Does it sound familiar? Write down an instance where this has happened and map out where your distractions took you, plus what time you lost with your partner. If it caused any larger consequences, write that down also. Being aware of your trail of distractions can help you redirect yourself when you recognize what is going on.

Agreed Upon Activity: _____

You get up and go to do something but then find the stream of distractions waiting for you.

What happens?

→ _____

→ _____

→ _____

→ _____

→ _____

→ _____

→ _____

→ _____

→ _____

→ _____

→ _____

→ _____

→ _____

How did things end up? _____

Did you get any consequences? _____

What could you have done differently? _____

Some tips to help:

- Talk things out.

- Do things that are interesting to both of you. Do not be afraid to try something new.

- Look at physical intimacy as an opportunity to mutually satisfy one another.

- Find professional help.

Your Relationship with Your Career

Building a career can be a tricky business.

Excuse the pun.

When you have ADHD, finding something that will hold your interest can be hard. If the task or project does not hold your attention, you may wind up quitting more jobs than you can list. Although working in an office seems like a good place to start your career, you may often feel restless or hate the thought of even going in. This may have you develop a work habit of long hours that may keep you staying late into the night or showing up earlier in the morning so you can focus and have quiet time to get work done.

If you hate your job, why do you work there?

You need money.

You cannot just fall into a "perfect" career.

What are some other reasons you work in the job you do?

The great thing about ADHD is that you can work a "pay the bills job" while seeking the job of your dreams. You have enough energy, strength, and creativity to work a full-time job, take care of a home, and pursue something you are passionate about. The most important question you need to ask yourself when thinking about your career is:

What do you really want to do?

Do not worry if you are not sure. There are many ways to find out what is right for you. Suppose you hear a little voice in your head telling you that something you want to do is not possible. Do not listen or tell it off. You are a creative, dynamic, multi-tasking machine. You can do anything (Davis & Hill, 2022).

Once you find the right pieces to your ADHD puzzle, you will be pretty much unstoppable.

Exercise Twenty-Eight: Find Your Chosen Career

Ask yourself the questions below. Answer them accordingly.

- What can you spend hours talking about or researching?

_____

_____

_____

_____

_____

_____

_____

- What would you prefer to do with your weekend time?

_____

_____

_____

_____

_____

_____

_____

● Can you work in a team, or do you choose to work individually?

_____

_____

_____

_____

_____

_____

_____

● Do you like to be in charge? Are you comfortable taking the lead?

_____

_____

_____

_____

_____

_____

_____

● What bothers you the most about people, places, and things (what are your pet peeves) (Davis & Hill, 2022)?

_____

_____

_____

_____

_____

_____

- Do you prefer fast- or slow-paced environments?

_____

_____

_____

_____

_____

_____

_____

- What activities drain you, and which ones excite you?

_____

_____

_____

_____

_____

_____

_____

- What job would you love to do if money wasn't an issue (Davis & Hill, 2022)?

_____

_____

_____

_____

_____

_____

_____

Now that you have a few answers, maybe some of the career ideas below can help grease the wheels of inspiration.

The Best Jobs for ADHD Minds are:

- Artist

- Athlete

- Beautician

- Chef

- Computer technician

- Copy editor

- Daycare worker

- Emergency Medical Technician (EMT), first responder

- Engineer

- Hair Stylist

- High-tech field

- Hospitality management or industry

- Journalist

- Nurse

- Sales representative (not in a call center)

- Small business owner

- Software engineer

- Stage management in the theater

- Teacher (Sheppard, 2021)

Do any of these sound like something you would like to do? If so, why don't you journal out a plan to get to where you want to be? If not, journal about some subjects you are most passionate about.

Your Relationship with Money

What is your relationship with money?

Do you avoid looking at your checking account?

Do you constantly forget where your bills are?

Are you unaware of how much credit card debt you have?

Are things okay and work well?

What are your money goals?

Exercise Twenty-Nine: What Are Your Goals?

Think about what you'd like your future with money to be. Include short-, mid-, and long-term goals. Make sure to include your partner or spouse if you have one (Davis & Hill, 2022).

Short-term goals examples are: Eat out less, keep financial documents organized, or save a specific amount of money each week.

Mid-term goal examples can be: going on vacation, buying new furniture, paying off one credit card, etc.

Long-term goal examples can be: building college savings or adding to your retirement funds.

Write these items below:

Short-term goals:

_____

_____

_____

_____

_____

_____

_____

_____

_____

Mid-term goals:

_____

_____

_____

_____

_____

_____

_____

_____

_____

Long-term goals:

_____

_____

_____

_____

_____

_____

_____

_____

_____

_____

Once you have a few ideas, you can create a vision board with images of items you would like to purchase in the future, or you can sort out your desired purchases into non-essentials and essential supplies (Davis & Hill, 2022). Answer the questions below to help:

What are the top three to five must-haves on your essential list?

_____

_____

_____

_____

_____

_____

_____

_____

_____

What are your top three to five must-haves on your non-essential list (Davis & Hill, 2022)?

_____

_____

_____

_____

_____

_____

_____

_____

_____

What is your current financial status?

_____

_____

_____

_____

_____

_____

_____

_____

_____

What is stopping you from having a healthy economic life?

_____

_____

_____

_____

_____

_____

_____

_____

_____

Where would you like to see yourself financially in one, three, and five years (Davis & Hill, 2022)?

_____

_____

_____

_____

_____

_____

_____

_____

_____

_____

Finding some problem spots in your spending habits can help you resolve some of the bigger money-related issues you have had. To develop successful money management, you must pay attention to the details. Each goal you set for your financial planning plays a vital role in your financial health.

If you find that you have impulse spending issues, review some tips below from the Women with ADHD companion book and see if they can help you curb your impulses.

Tips for taming your impulses:

- Click 'unsubscribe.' These darn emails send a bunch of sales and specials to your inbox.

- Keep track of what you spend while you shop.

- Learn what your temptations are, and come up with a plan to stay away from them.

- Look for things to do locally that are free or inexpensive.

- Make things a little harder on yourself. Keep the credit cards at home. Bring the lowest amount of money you think you will need.

- Find an amount of time that feels right, like twenty-four hours, and wait to purchase your item. If, after time passes, you have the money and still want the bigger object, then you can buy it.

- Use a shopping list and stick to the items on it.

- Vulnerability leads to that needed dose of dopamine, and when you are shopping, that can be a super trigger. If you find yourself shopping in an emotional mood, returning to the task later is best when you feel more grounded and focused.

Conclusion

Throughout this chapter, you took a quick pass through your social, career, and financial relationships. While these are not an extensive list of places you can go, they are all good exercise and tips on where you can start. Hopefully, with time, practice, and help from others, you will find yourself getting into a good pattern with friends, romance, and finances. Also, keep looking for the job you are most passionate about. You deserve to love what you do and to do what you love.

The next chapter will discuss health, exercise, and ADHD mind-body tips and tricks.

CHAPTER SEVEN

ADHD, Health & Exercise

Introduction

Treating your body and mind well helps keep your body and mind working in the most efficient way they can. This chapter will discuss a few of those items and give tips and tricks on eating and treating yourself well to be well.

Healthy Eating

Factually, no significant data has connected ADHD with what you eat. However, research indicates that certain foods and vitamins help your brain and body function smoother than without whole foods.

Neurologically, foods rich in protein help build connections between neurotransmitters, which means your brain will have a better foundation for more streamlined communication.

Examples of Protein-Rich Foods

- Beans
- Eggs
- Fish
- Nuts
- Poultry

Examples of Vitamins and Minerals

Zinc, iron, and magnesium have been shown to regulate neurotransmitters and level out cognitive differences. Regular incorporation of zinc into your diet will encourage dopamine regulation, calming your brain. Magnesium will refocus and relax your brain, whereas low iron levels have been shown to correlate with cognitive issues (Muhammad, 2022; Davis & Hill, 2022).

Statements about food in the Women with ADHD companion book are as follows:

"Foods high on the Glycemic Index (GI) can release rapid glucose, increasing inattention, hyperactivity, and impulsivity. Processed foods like artificial dyes and white, refined sugars have a poor connection with brain activity. They are generally recommended to steer clear from when you have any sort of neurological disruption.

If you get knowledgeable about reading the labels on your food packages, you'll be able to learn the foods to stay away from and which ones are good for you. Words like: dehydrated cane juice, dextrin, dextrose, high-fructose corn sweetener, maltodextrin, molasses, malt syrup, and sucrose are all code words for sugar (Davis & Hill, 2022; Muhammad, 2022)."

Healthy Foods to Eat

- **Artichokes**—this vegetable supports the function of the liver. The liver detoxes the body, and adding artichokes can boost that process. They are also high in fiber, which promotes lower-hormone levels for when your levels may be riding a little high. When you have higher or too high hormone levels, your body will produce more cortisol and estrogen, which can increase breast chance in certain individuals.

Foods high in fiber digest slowly so you will feel fuller longer and help you maintain healthy energy levels throughout your day (Azzaro, 2021).

- **Broccoli**—this vegetable is in a group called cruciferous. Broccoli is rich in glucosinolates like kale, cabbage, Brussels sprouts, and cauliflower. This compound helps eliminate and neutralize carcinogens, indole-three-cabriole, and isothiocyanates, which are nutrients to help prevent estrogen-related cancers.

Broccoli is a vegetable high in fiber and assists in removing excess estrogen through bowel movements (Nutrition, 2022).

- **Flaxseeds**—this seed contains lignans, which is a plant-based, estrogen-like substance and weaker than the estrogen that your body makes. The benefits include healthy hormone levels by creating longer luteal phases (the second part of your menstrual cycle), lowering estrogen and testosterone levels, reducing breast pain, and preventing postmenopausal breast cancer.

Flax seeds are also high in fiber (Azzaro, 2021).

Fresh Herbs—aromatic herbs like garlic, ginger and turmeric, basil, oregano, parsley, and thyme are ripe with nutritious phytochemicals that can benefit your health (Azzaro, 2021).

- **Lentils**—like salmon and artichokes, lentils are a slow-burning protein, which means you will feel fuller longer. They are also an amazing source of fiber, protein, and zinc. Lentils can reduce estrogen levels and raise testosterone (Nutrition, 2022).

- **Salmon**—this fish is a good source of omega-three fatty acids and vitamin E, which are great bases for anti-inflammatory healing. Salmon also contains cholesterol. Cholesterol is the main ingredient that helps make hormones. It is a waxy substance in all cells that helps create cholesterol. Although different foods have cholesterol, you will want to eat plenty of food with HDL (high-density lipoproteins) and stay away from LDL (low-density lipoproteins). Low-density lipoproteins leave deposits of plaque in your arteries and create blockages. High-density lipoproteins will carry the plaque out of your arteries (Younkin, 2021).

Because salmon is an anti-inflammatory food, it will help reduce menstrual cramping, lower the production of stress hormones, and help alleviate cortisol levels.

The protein in salmon digest slower than in other food, which means you will have a satisfying feeling for longer after you eat it (Azzaro, 2021).

- **Shrimp and Shellfish**—examples of this food include scallops, clams, and shrimp.

This type of seafood has an abundance of good minerals like iodine, zinc, and selenium, which are vital to a properly functioning thyroid. Although in a much lower dose than salmon, these foods also contain many omega-three fatty acids and act as anti-inflammatory.

Shrimp, muscles, scallops, etc., contain EPA, DHA, and tryptophan, which encourage the production of melatonin in the body, a crucial hormone for good sleep (Azzaro, 2021).

- **Sunflower Seeds**—are rich in vitamin E, an antioxidant important to estrogen, and boost progesterone, too (Nutrition, 2022).

- **Sweet Potatoes**—this type of tuber is high in vitamin B6 and helps your body by detoxifying the liver. Any foods that aid by detoxing your liver assists in ridding extra hormones. Chicken, turkey, and spinach are other foods plentiful with vitamin B6 (Nutrition, 2022).

- **Organic Tempeh**—organic soy has positive effects that come from isoflavones. Isoflavones have phytoestrogen properties that help reduce the risk of breast cancer and can increase probiotics when eaten with a fermentation agent (Nutrition, 2022).

For Adrenal Hormones

If you find that you have adrenal fatigue or that it is hyperactive, you can eat some of the food below to help you balance out any issues and give your medication a boost.

- **Almonds**—contain healthy fats to help balance blood sugar, support nervous system function, and reduce inflammation.

- **Avocado**—has a spectrum of healthy fats to keep blood sugar levels even and supports proper nervous system functionality. Avocado contains vitamin B5, which helps fight stress (Nutrition, 2022).

- **Bell Peppers**—green, red, yellow, and orange bell peppers are sweet and full of vitamin C. This vitamin is an antioxidant essential to a good functioning adrenal gland. Foods that are high in vitamin C will replenish, reduce stress levels, and give you a nice energy boost.

- **Eggs**—will boost your choline, a vitamin that assists in the production of the neurotransmitter acetylcholine. This vitamin is crucial to helping your brain, nervous system, memory, and development function well. When you buy organic, pasture-raised eggs, you will get a nice dose of omega-three fatty acids, which also aid in reducing inflammation.

- **Kale**—while not in the cruciferous family, kale is a dark, leafy green that provides various nutrients like vitamins K, A, and C. Kale has similar traits to bell peppers as it brings in extra antioxidants to help with stress reduction.

- **Millet**—contains a variety of B vitamins to support the nervous system and reduce stress. It is also whole grain and gluten-free. With extra fiber and magnesium to boot, it will help balance your blood sugar levels.

- **Pumpkin Seeds**—these seeds are rich in magnesium, which works in tandem with vitamins C and B5. This type of seed will lower stress levels and help us relax.

- **Sea Salt**—when you are depleted of the hormone aldosterone, you will crave salt. However, this generally means that your adrenal glands are not working either. When you add sea salt to your food or even a glass of water, you will replenish your levels and bump up the balance in your fluid and blood pressure (Nutrition, 2022).

For Thyroid Hormones

Thyroid issues are a problem that has not been completely figured out due to the complex nature of your thyroid. If it works well, you will not notice a difference, but if it is out of balance, you can become hypo or hyper-. Neither of these thyroid problems is good for your body, and while medication usually is an important part of the healing process, some tests may not show that you have an issue. However, if you notice a drastic change in weight and energy, you could have an imbalance that does not show up on tests. See some helpful food below that can give you a place to start feeling better.

- **Brazil Nuts**—these nuts are ripe with selenium, which is an antioxidant that converts T4 into T3, an active form of a thyroid hormone. T3 is needed for your thyroid to work well, but selenium also produces your gland.

- **Quinoa**—is a seed and a superfood. This seed has a ton of fiber, minerals, and protein. It is a slow-burning food that allows you to feel fuller longer and will help you with constipation which a slow thyroid will bring.

- **Sardines**—this small fish with a sordid reputation is chock-full of B12, selenium, and iodine. These nutrients are all needed to support your thyroid healthily.

- **Seaweed**—is a vegetable of the sea. You may also find it under other names like arame, dulse, hijiki, kombu, nori, wakame, and more. Seaweed is a great place to find iodine, a vital mineral in the production of thyroid hormones.

- **Spinach**—is amazing vegetation that helps enhance thyroid function and hormones and boosts energy. Spinach is rich in iron, B vitamins, and fiber (Nutrition, 2022).

Exercise

When thinking about exercise, it's best to find something that you like to do. If you're not a huge fan of exercise, start with walking because exercise is crucial to help your ADHD brain to "focus, burn energy, and relieve yourself of some of those peskier symptoms like impulsivity and inattention (Davis & Hill, 2022)."

Exercise improves memory function, blood flow, learning abilities, brain plasticity, retention of new mental and physical skills, and how your brain cells communicate with one another. You will also see a boost in your mood because each time you exercise you get a swift kick of dopamine to your brain, which will feel similar to the instant gratification high that you get when you react impulsively (Basso & Suzuki, 2017).

Some of the best exercises for ADHD are below. After you exercise, it's recommended that your journal about how you feel and think so you can see how things are different for you (Preiato, 2021):

- Bicycling

- Spinning

- Jogging

- Hiking

- Browning

- Elliptical

- Boxing

- Martial arts

- HIIT (high-intensity interval training)

- CrossFit

- Weightlifting

ADHD has many symptoms, including mental burnout that causes impulsivity and inattention. Exercises and activities above will help avoid burnout from your ADHD symptoms.

Conclusion

This chapter discussed how healthy eating and exercise could help work out some of your ADHD symptoms and give you more focus and a less foggy ADHD brain. When you include exercises, even walking, into your daily routine, you will attain better memory, blood flow, ability to learn, retention of psychical and mental skills, and brain plasticity. Your mood will also get steadier, and brain cells will communicate more clearly (Basso & Suzuki, 2017).

CONCLUSION

Rewriting the ADHD Script

With everything in this workbook, you have the tools to write your own ADHD script. You are an amazing individual with many incredible qualities. Although ADHD will give you some bumps and bruises along the way, you can challenge each one, flourish, and find the best version of yourself.

Thank You

Before you leave, I'd just like to say, thank you so much for purchasing my book.

I spent many days and nights working on this book so I could finally put this in your hands.

So, before you leave, I'd like to ask you a small favor.

Would you please consider posting a review on the platform? Your reviews are one of the best ways to support indie authors like me, and every review counts.

Your feedback will allow me to continue writing books just like this one, so let me know if you enjoyed it and why. I read every review and I would love to hear from you.

References

"ADHD in Women 101." Kaleidoscope Society, www.kaleidoscopesociety.com/adhd-in-women-101. Accessed 12 Aug. 2022.

Alloway, T. P., and R. G. Alloway. "Investigating the Predictive Roles of Working Memory and IQ in Academic Attainment." Journal of Experimental Child Psychology, 2010, p. 106 (1), https://doi.org/10.1016/j.jecp.2009.11.003.

Azzaro, M. R. G. (2021, September 9). The Best Foods for Hormone Health, According to a Dietitian. EatingWell. https://www.eatingwell.com/article/7917059/best-foods-for-hormone-health-according-to-a-dietitian/

Bailey, Eileen, and ADDitude's Adhd Medical Review Panel. "Executive Dysfunction Test: Symptoms in Adults with ADHD." ADDitude, 6 June 2022, www.additudemag.com/executive-function-deficit-adhd-symptoms-test-for-adults/?src=embed_link.

Barker, Randolph T., et al. "Preliminary Investigation of Employee's Dog Presence on Stress and Organizational Perceptions." International Journal of Workplace Health Management, vol. 5, no. 1, 2012, pp. 15–30. Crossref, https://doi.org/10.1108/17538351211215366.

Barker, Sandra B., et al. "A Randomized Cross-over Exploratory Study of the Effect of Visiting Therapy Dogs on College Student Stress Before Final Exams." Anthrozoös, vol. 29, no. 1, 2016, pp. 35–46. Crossref, https://doi.org/10.1080/08927936.2015.1069988.

Barkley, Russell, PhD, and Michele Novotni PhD. "What Is Executive Function? 7 Deficits Tied to ADHD." ADDitude, 10 Aug. 2022, www.additudemag.com/7-executive-function-deficits-linked-to-adhd.

Barth, C., Villringer, A., & Sacher, J. (2015). Sex hormones affect neurotransmitters and shape the adult female brain during hormonal transition periods. Frontiers in Neuroscience, 9. https://doi.org/10.3389/fnins.2015.00037

Basso, J. C., & Suzuki, W. A. (2017). The Effects of Acute Exercise on Mood, Cognition, Neurophysiology, and Neurochemical Pathways: A Review. Brain Plasticity, 2(2), 127–152. https://doi.org/10.3233/bpl-160040

rtin, Mark, MD. "Calm Starts at Home: How to Teach Emotional Regulation Skills." ADDitude, 7 Apr. 2022, www.additudemag.com/emotional-regulation-skills-adhd-children.

roadbent, E. (2022, February 10). 5 Ways ADHD Makes Me the Best, Rudest, Most Caring, Totally Frustrating Friend You'll Ever Have. ADDitude. https://www.additudemag.com/your-adhd-friend/

Cantrell, T. (2022, January 28). The Most Genius Tips for Organizing and Cleaning with ADHD. Little Miss Lionheart. https://littlemisslionheart.com/how-to-conquer-the-clutter-when-you-have-adhd/

CHADD. (2018, May 8). ADHD Complicates Romance. https://chadd.org/adhd-weekly/adhd-complicates-romance/

CHADD. (12–12). The Secret Lives of Girls with ADHD. http://drellenlittman.com/secret_life_of_girls_with_adhd.pdf

Cooper, C. B., Neufeld, E. V., Dolezal, B. A., & Martin, J. L. (2018). Sleep deprivation and obesity in adults: a brief narrative review. BMJ Open Sport & Exercise Medicine, 4(1), e000392. https://doi.org/10.1136/bmjsem-2018-000392

Connolly, Maureen, and Sharon Psy. D. Saline. "ADHD in Girls: The Symptoms That Are Ignored in Females." ADDitude, 15 July 2022, www.additudemag.com/adhd-in-girls-women.

Davis, Sarah, and Linda Hill. Women with ADHD: The Complete Guide to Stay Organized, Overcome Distractions, and Improve Relationships. Manage Your Emotions, Finances, and Succeed in Life. Independently published, 2022.

Diamond, Adele, PhD. "How to Sharpen Executive Functions: Activities to Hone Brain Skills." ADDitude, 19 July 2022, www.additudemag.com/how-to-improve-executive-function-adhd.

Dua, K. (2022, April 11). 24 Bullet Journal Period Tracker Layouts and Ideas For You. The Creatives Hour. https://thecreativeshour.com/period-tracker-bullet-journal/

"Executive Function Fact Sheet." LD OnLine, www.ldonline.org/ld-topics/teaching-instruction/executive-function-fact-sheet. Accessed 29 Aug. 2022.

Gatti, Claudia. "Women with ADHD." ADHD Online, 3 Aug. 2022, adhdonline.com/women-with-adhd.

Gee, N. R., et al. "Preschoolers Make Fewer Errors on an Object Categorization Task in the Presence of a Dog." Anthrozoös, 2010, pp. 23, 223–30, https://doi.org/10.2752/175303710X12750451258896.

Green, Rachel, and Dr. Rachel Colemen. "ADHD Symptom Spotlight: Emotional Dysregulation." Verywell Mind, 28 Feb. 2022, www.verywellmind.com/adhd-symptom-spotlight-emotional-dysregulation-5219946.

References

Hendry, Alexandra, et al. "Executive Function in the First Three Years of Life: Precurso Predictors and Patterns." Developmental Review, vol. 42, 2016, pp. 1–33. Crossr https://doi.org/10.1016/j.dr.2016.06.005.

Jaksa, Peter, PhD. "How to Regain Your Confidence: Life-Changing Strategies for Adults wi ADHD." ADDitude, 1 July 2022, www.additudemag.com/how-to-regain-self-confidence adults-adhd.

Kessler, Ronald C., and Kathleen R. Merikangas. "The National Comorbidity Survey Replication (NCS-R): Background and Aims." International Journal of Methods in Psychiatric Research, vol. 13, no. 2, 2004, pp. 60–68. Crossref, https://doi.org/10.1002/mpr.166.

Lang, A. B. (2022, January 31). 10 Natural Ways to Balance Your Hormones. Healthline. https://www.healthline.com/nutrition/balance-hormones

Main, Beth. "ADHD and Setting SMART Goals." ADDitude, 29 July 2021, www.additudemag.com/adhd-and-setting-smart-goals.

McCarthy, L. F., & Novotni, M., PhD. (2022, July 11). Women, Hormones, and ADHD. ADDitude. https://www.additudemag.com/women-hormones-and-adhd/

Muhammad, R. (2022, February 1). ADHD Online Foods & ADHD: Is there a link? ADHD Online. https://adhdonline.com/foods-adhd-is-there-a-link/

Nadeau, K. M., & Quinn, P. O. (2002). Understanding Women with AD/HD (Updated ed.). Advantage Books.

National Institute Of Neurological Disorders And Stroke. "Brain Basics: Understanding Sleep | National Institute of Neurological Disorders and Stroke." Https://Www.Ninds.Nih.Gov, www.ninds.nih.gov/health-information/patient-caregiver-education/brain-basics-understanding-sleep?msclkid=2a4be251b60e11eca6796c8b48d06f4a#6. Accessed 14 Aug. 2022.

Novotni, M., PhD. (2022, February 10). "I Feel Utterly, Hopelessly Alone." ADDitude. https://www.additudemag.com/feeling-socially-weak-build-your-strength/

Nutrition, A. O. C. (2022, July 27). 20 Best Hormone Balancing Foods and Meal Plans! Academy of Culinary Nutrition. https://www.culinarynutrition.com/20-best-hormone-balancing-foods/

Preiato, R. D. D. (2021, October 19). Exploring the Link Between ADHD and Exercise. Healthline. https://www.healthline.com/health/fitness/adhd-and-exercise#exercise-and-adhd

Price-Mitchell Ph.D., M. "Goal-Setting Is Linked to Higher Achievement." Psychology Today, Psychology Today, 14 Mar. 2018, www.psychologytoday.com/us/blog/the-moment-youth/201803/goal-setting-is-linked-higher-achievement.

uinn, Patricia. "Perceptions of Girls and ADHD: Results from a National Survey." edGenMed, vol. 6 (2), no. 2, 2004, pubmed.ncbi.nlm.nih.gov/15266229.

ollins, K. (2019, September 20). You Can Call Me Ms. Clean. ADDitude. ttps://www.additudemag.com/household-cleaning-and-organization/

haw, Philip, et al. "Emotion Dysregulation in Attention Deficit Hyperactivity Disorder." American Journal of Psychiatry, vol. 171, no. 3, 2014, pp. 276–93. Crossref, https://doi.org/10.1176/appi.ajp.2013.13070966.

Sheppard, S. (2021, October 3). Here are the Best Jobs for People With ADHD. Verywell Mind. https://www.verywellmind.com/the-best-jobs-for-people-with-adhd-5201906

Sreenivas, Shishira. "ADHD in Women." WebMD, 24 Mar. 2021, www.webmd.com/add-adhd/adhd-in-women?msclkid=5b6be0cab6ad11ecb5e728f6cbc04ef0.

Stewart, Becca. "Setting Goals with the SMART Method." Winning Agent, 23 Sept. 2021, www.winningagent.com/smart-method.

"What Is ADHD?" Centers for Disease Control and Prevention, 26 Jan. 2021, www.cdc.gov/ncbddd/adhd/facts.html?msclkid=f6e557acb52a11ec93ffbafa5b85d79c.

"---." Psychiatry.Org, Psychiatry, www.psychiatry.org/patients-families/adhd/what-is-adhd?msclkid=f6e5eb7bb52a11ecbcb083b6e32b632e. Accessed 13 Aug. 2022.

"Why Do We Sleep, Anyway? | Healthy Sleep." Http://Healthysleep.Med.Harvard.Edu, healthysleep.med.harvard.edu/healthy/matters/benefits-of-sleep/why-do-we-sleep?msclkid=2a4b31abb60e11ec8e2dfc2c9b6e6531. Accessed 14 Aug. 2022.

Young, W. F., Jr. (2022, August 24). Overview of the Endocrine System. Merck Manuals Professional Edition. https://www.merckmanuals.com/professional/endocrine-and-metabolic-disorders/principles-of-endocrinology/overview-of-the-endocrine-system

Younkin, M. L. S. (2021, August 17). What You Need to Know About Your Cholesterol Levels. EatingWell. https://www.eatingwell.com/article/7877576/what-you-need-to-know-about-your-cholesterol-levels/